Bishop Quander Lear Wilson, Sr.

A Man Before His Time

Bishop Edward E. Shouse, Sr., DD

A MAN BEFORE HIS TIME

First Printing: October 2020
Printed in the United States of America

Published by:
Executive Business Writing
P.O. Box 10002
Moreno Valley, CA 92552
(951)268-0365
www.executivebusinesswriting.org
Editors: Dr. Beverly Crockett and Mrs. Julie Boney
Book cover: Mrs. Tracy Spencer - Legacy Media, LLC Sketch
Artist: Mr. Gregory Hawkins

TABLE OF CONTENTS

FOREWORD

Bishop Edward E. Shouse, Sr., has captured the essence of all that was known about our beloved Bishop Quander Lear Wilson, Sr., known to most of us as "Pappy." In this book you will find yourself laughing, crying, and remembering the good and the bad times.

All who knew Bishop Wilson will find themselves somewhere in the pages of this story about him, this luminous man of God. Bishop Shouse has reached back in time and has unveiled the subject on "A Man Before His Time."

Bishop Shouse was raised by Bishop and Mother Wilson. However, many of us who were close to Bishop Wilson feel as if we were raised by him also. That's why we all loved him and called him Pappy.

As you read this book, you will know that Bishop Shouse did not pull any punches; instead he has told the story of a man whom many did not understand, simply because he was truly a man ahead of his time.

I remember the times as if they were yesterday that Bishop Wilson would say, "Son, the day will come…" and he would reveal what that day would be, and just as sure as I am living today, many of those days did come.

What an honor and privilege to have known Bishop Quander Lear Wilson, Sr., the man who was before his time.

The late Bishop Kenneth L. Lisath, Th.M., Senior Pastor
New Jerusalem Christian Center, Ironton, Ohio

DEDICATION

This book is dedicated to the memory of my late parents, Bishop Quander Lear Wilson, Sr., and Mother Mary Helen Wilson, along with all the many sons and daughters that my father birthed spiritually.

Thanks and all my love to my beautiful wife, my soulmate, Rose Marie, my daughters Loretta and Anissa, and my son, Edward, Jr., for having the confidence in me and providing the encouragement to help me complete this book.

This manuscript is also dedicated to all of my spiritual brothers and sisters; some who are of great renown, and those who may not yet have the spotlight on them but are still striving to be all that God has called them to be.

We understand and know that Bishop's mantle was torn in pieces and distributed to all of us at various times in our lives and ministries. How blessed we are to have known and loved this gentle giant, one of the apostolic fathers of our time. May those who read this book have pleasant memories of our bishop and spiritual father, and those who had not the opportunity to do so be enlightened and tremendously blessed by the words herein.

With love and respect,
Bishop Edward E. Shouse, Sr., DD

DISCLAIMER

The information contained in this book is not meant to embarrass or cause any problems to any person, whether dead or alive, but as an enlightening source of information concerning the late Bishop Quander L. Wilson, Sr.

References to events, circumstances, and situations are actual happenings. However, although no attempt to name specific persons is intended, some events, circumstances, people, and situations may be recognized by the readers. In other words, you may recognize yourself.

The opinions, statements, events, and ideas expressed and described by this writer are that solely of the writer and not meant to be offensive to the readers.

All information given concerning Bishop Quander Lear Wilson, Sr., his family, events, family history, and origin of the Quander family and its name, is gathered from sources given to this writer during the lifetime of Bishop Wilson and is used by his permission given before his death.

ACKNOWLEDGEMENTS

To serve a general in the Kingdom of God is quite an honor to be bestowed upon men and women. For there, many deposits, interactions, impartations, and transfers take place. The very word ministry means 'to serve,' as was taught by Chief Prelate, Bishop Quander L. Wilson, Sr. To even find oneself in the position of serving is truly humbling, and though it should be that we all submit to it, that is not always the case.

Throughout the life and times of ministry and greatness of Bishop Wilson, there were many who served as adjutants, personal caregivers, drivers, and aides to him. To name them all would take many pages of this book. At various times, there may have been one, and at other times there was a quorum, each serving in a unique capacity.

I would like to give special recognition to my son, Bishop Edward E. "EJ" Shouse, Jr., who from a young man until Bishop's passing, served him tirelessly and received numerous untold apostolic deposits from the man of God, his grandfather; to Elder Frank Watkins, Elder William "BB" Hamby, Minister Timothy Hendricks, Bishop Timothy Lynch, Bishop Stephen White, and last but certainly not least, to my daughters Elder Loretta and Elder Anissa Shouse.

If by chance I failed to mention someone, please note that it is not intentional, but know that there are scores of men and women who served the bishop over the years. Your labor of love does not go unnoticed, especially by the Lord. I say to you, thank you and may the Lord reward you accordingly. For the Word of God says, "He that receiveth a prophet in the name of a prophet shall receive a prophet's reward; and he that receiveth a righteous man in the name of a righteous man shall receive a righteous man's reward." Matthew 10:41

INTRODUCTION

Bishop. T. D Jakes, Bishop Q. L. Wilson
Bishop. E. E. Shouse, Sr.
Bishop. E. M. Wortham

In the passing of time, and in all of our lives, there will be that one person who touches lives, changes lives, and makes such an impact on those who come in contact with them. In these writings, I will endeavor to highlight a few of the events that I experienced with this great man of God. I was blessed to know him as a pastor, father, and great friend.

I want to start off by saying that I will be comparing Bishop Wilson with some Biblical characters as well as some characters who were known centuries later in the secular world.

King David, as recorded in Psalm 37:37, said, "Mark the perfect man and behold the upright: for the end of that man is peace." To have known Bishop Wilson is to have loved him, he made such a lasting impression on those he met until one would never forget him. If you never had the opportunity to meet him, read along with me and you will see the impression I am speaking about.

History has recorded the life and writings of the early century prophet, Nostradamus. Per Wikipedia, Michel de Nostredame (depending on the source, 14 or 21 December 1503 – 1 or 2 July 1566), usually Latinized as Nostradamus, was a French astrologer, physician, and reputed seer, who is best known for his book, Les Prophéties, a collection of 942 poetic quatrains, allegedly predicting future events. The book was first published in 1555 and has rarely been out of print since his death.

On occasion I have heard it said that he was one who was before his time. Nostradamus wrote the things he saw in his time in 10 volumes and in groups of 100, in what were called quatrains (Quatrains of Nostradamus: Nostradamus completed a total of 942 quatrains, which he organized into centuries - groups of 100 quatrains. One century had only 42 quatrains. A quatrain is simply a poem with 4 lines.)

To this day, the things he saw and recorded hold our attention vividly. As you read his account of various things he saw in his lifetime and in the future, you will find it so amazing that his writings are still being investigated to see what made this man so phenomenal.

I am one who believes that things in life don't just happen, but that they happen for a reason. So it was with the late Bishop Quander L. Wilson, Sr. He, like Nostradamus, saw many things in the future, and because he saw things and events that directly affected people, he reached out to people and offered hope to so many people in their time of despair.

During and throughout all of his theological training and ministry, the Lord planted the seed of His Word in Bishop Wilson, which seemed to sprout many branches as he walked with the Lord. Down through the years, this holy seed that was growing in him by the power of the Holy Spirit enabled him to build amazing bridges across many denominational walls that had been severed by mankind. There was not a place that he could go and not be accepted, from storefront churches to great cathedrals. Not only did he sit amongst fellow ministers, but at one time he was summoned to sit with one of our past presidents. He would always say, "The president needs to know and have God too."

It was no secret that Bishop Wilson spoke many refreshing words into people's lives, which in turn helped scores of souls find salvation and deliverance. The fruit of his labor can be seen and heard through the voices of many in ministry today.

Some of what we are hearing in this hour from many great men and women of God was heard years ago through the voice of Bishop, that came straight from the throne of God. Some of us are not surprised at the revelation of God's Word today, because he would impart certain things into our spirits. He would take the time and pour into us, and for that reason we are what we are and where we are today. We did not understand everything he said, but we knew that he had heard from the Lord.

He proved time and time again that if one would spend time with the Lord, one would receive not only vision, but also the revelation of God's Word. What an expositor and visionary of God's Word, who had a way of leading and pushing others to the top, while seemingly being left standing in the shadows.

There is truth to the scripture, "Write the vision and make it plain upon tables, that he may run that readeth it." Bishop always wanted to take somebody with him as he traveled in the spiritual realm.

I have planted, Apollos watered;
but God gave the increase.
I Corinthians 3:6

Chapter 1

MAN CHILD

Carrie & George Wilson - Bishop Wilson's Parents

When George Cummings Burtis Wilson married Carrie Ella Quander on the 13th day of September, 1896, at Port Kennedy, Pennsylvania, they had no idea they were going to bring a life into the world whose steps would be ordered by the Lord and would also would be a man before his time.

The Lord moves in mysterious ways. This last son born to George and Carrie Wilson was referred to, as we often say in this day and time, as a change-of-life baby. This was said because his mother was past the time of having a baby, according to man's standards. This son came into the world and was blessed to be given his mother's maiden name as his first name, which in itself was different. But similar to the biblical story of Abraham and Sarah, this was an uncommon birth. I don't know whether Mother Carrie laughed as did Sarah, but there may had been some laughter over the whole matter.

If it were possible, it would be interesting to hear the comments from his late parents concerning him. They certainly were surprised but blessed by his arrival. My father and I would often talk and he would tell me that he was the way he was because he was a change-of-life baby.

From his birth on July 4th, 1918, in Berwyn, Pennsylvania, to his promotion to Glory from this world on March 23, 2003 in Columbus, Ohio, he made such an impact on all those with whom he came in contact. I can imagine as a baby he must have been a beautiful baby. Bishop Wilson grew up in the Philadelphia, Pennsylvania area, attended the Mt. Pleasant Elementary School System, and graduated from Radnor High School with the class of 1936.

Perhaps we can say about him as King David said about himself, "I am fearfully and wonderfully made." We who knew Bishop Wilson knew him to be a handsome, stately gentleman with a million-dollar smile and a personality to match.

As he would often tell me, he always knew he would be different from the rest of his siblings. Coming from an incredibly talented family that included an array of musicians, preachers, and wood workers, just to name a few of the prevalent occupations in his family, surely this man was before his time. He could take the crudest things and produce something positive. I have seen him do mechanical work with a limited number of tools, making do and improvising with others, to fix whatever needed to be fixed.

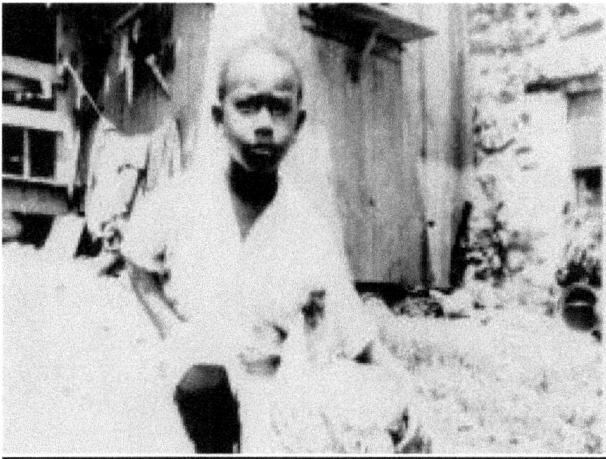

Bishop Wilson as a child with his pet chicken

Man Child

Chapter 2

PREACHER BEFORE HIS TIME

The steps of a good man are ordered by the Lord.
Psalm 37:23

I understand that no man is perfect, as it is written in the Bible, "all have sinned and come short of the glory of God." In his natural life, I observed Bishop trying his best to please God and to please those with whom was called to serve. Let me show you here a man who was after God's own heart.

Bishop Wilson taught that when the Lord has His hands on your life, there is a divine purpose for your life and nothing is going to take you out until that divine purpose is fulfilled. He believed and taught that regardless of what circumstances you may be born into, and regardless of who your parents may be, the Lord would obtain from you what His purpose was for you.

I often listened to him speak of his growing up years. He could easily have gotten on the road to destruction, or he could have been a star in the shining light, glitz, and glamor of Broadway. He had all the qualifications. He was incredibly talented, handsome, and had an award-winning personality to match. He was a great musician, singer, orator, and communicator, but the Lord had other plans for his life and called him into ministry, where he was blessed to be a preacher of the Gospel of Jesus Christ.

He was one who had the ability to preach to the masses as well as smaller crowds and hold their interest while doing so. Those of us who came up under his ministry and teachings witnessed this over the years, as students under his tutelage in ministry.

He certainly was called to preach and could expound on anything. He taught many of us to find a sermon in everything, something that has helped this preacher down through the years. I in turn, have taught and am still teaching those I am responsible for to do the same. Get a message out of everything, for if you look closely enough, the Lord puts a message in all of our circumstances, situations, and just everyday living.

With all the cards stacked in place for him to gain acclaim as a Broadway star, he chose to follow the path laid out by the Lord. As a young man, I heard him preach many sermons. One of many that stand out in my mind is "Funky Broadway." He actually took a text from the writings of King Solomon and brought to life the story of a young man who went out on the, "Broadway of the Bible" and ended up facing the many temptations much like the Broadway we know of today.

He had a wit about himself to turn heads, to get one's attention. If only you could have been there when he announced that subject, "Funky Broadway!" Of course, he had it all fixed up for the "deep saints" and for those like me, who didn't care what the subject was. We just wanted to hear what he had to say. When he announced his subject, "Funky Broadway," there was a lot of whispering and hunching in the sides of the people in the pews. Ribs were nearly broken, and I know many were sore from the elbows that were given to make people pay attention to the subject. Of course, many faces had smirks on them, but being the kind of man he was, he held his ground. When he got finished telling us about how people wanted the bright lights and good times, including some of the church folk, and giving his detailed description of the woman who stood on the street corner and lured the young man into her bedroom and kept him there until the pain the young man felt was like an arrow piercing his liver, there were a whole lot of amens. And those who had the smirks on their faces could do nothing but get with him and receive the message. As many of you know, Bishop Wilson could say some things that nobody else could say and get away with, and in his later years he would say something witty and then tell the people, "I'm too old to worry about it," and go on with his message.

The Prophet

As I travel back and forth to the place where I was raised, one of his most vivid prophecies stands clear to me. It was years ago that he stood on the porch of his home in the southern part of Ohio, a little town called Burlington, and prophesied that industry and commerce would come to that particular area. Many didn't believe him.

I remember him trying to convince Mother Wilson to let him buy up the property that was lying dormant. At that time, it was all weeds and underbrush, and not very attractive at all. It was actually swamp land, for water would lay in the low-lying places for days. For whatever reason, she did not agree. To keep peace in the household, he let the chance to buy the land pass by. But now when I return and look at what was once swamp and underbrush, I see that unattractive land is now a bustling shopping mall, with much business and commerce going on. Oh yes, I cannot but wonder what would have been the outcome had he had his way and bought up the land.

The Author

As I read the writings of Bishop Wilson, especially those found in his book, *Created by Design,* in which he describes some of his own characteristics, I believe he was inspired to speak about man being created by design in the Lord's scheme of things. I am sure he used some of his own life's experiences as well as revelation from the Word of God in putting together so many examples of situations that man has experienced. If one were to read his book, you could hear him speak plainly concerning life.

In some ways, life gave him a challenge. The enemy tried to take him out on more than one occasion. In one instance, he shared how his head got caught in an elevator. The fact that he survived such a traumatic experience was a miracle. As you know, there are not many people around who have had their head caught in a moving elevator and lived to tell the story.

Saying that Bishop Wilson was a man before his time is a true statement to me, as I personally have been a witness to many of his prophecies coming to pass.

The Name

There is something about a name. I often caution young parents to seek the meaning of the name they are considering naming their children to know what it actually means.

Let us take a look at the last name, Quander, which would become the first name of Bishop Wilson. Research of that name uncovers remarkable history. It can be found linked to slavery; also, it can be found linked to the first president of the United States, George Washington, who is often referred to as the father of our nation.

I chuckle when I visit the home of President George Washington in Mount Vernon, Virginia, and see all the history and artifacts that are on display. When I listen to the stories that are told concerning the slaves, I want to stand up and tell the guide about one of those descendants who is not mentioned, that being Bishop Quander L. Wilson, Sr.

I did some research from some of the information Bishop Wilson had given me on the name, Quander, and found the name had and still has, a connection with the Cape Coast region of Ghana, West Africa. My research further revealed that from the 1800's until now, there have been many spellings and pronunciations of it, and many have been named, honoring it. In my years, I know of several who bear the name of Quander. Of course, the name is altered to fit the gender.

I am blessed to have a grandson named after him, Quander Lear Shouse, the second child of my son, Edward, Jr. My hope for my grandson is that he becomes as great or greater than his great-grandfather.

The Quander name has deep African roots, yet it can trace its roots in the United States all the way back to the nation's capital in Washington, DC. and the surrounding suburb of Alexandria, Virginia. Streets are named after the Quander family from there all the way down to George Washington's Mt. Vernon estate, where it is widely known that slaves were owned by this nation's first president.

As a matter of fact, you can still see the slave quarters on the tour of President Washington's estate. It has been said there was one slave who found favor in President Washington's eyes by the name of Mary Quander. She became the nexus that made the Quander family linked directly to this nation's first president.

These are facts that somehow were overlooked and would never have come to light until someone took the time to research and was able to bring them to the forefront. By the way, President George Washington was not the only U.S. president who had favorite slaves, thus producing relatives who were not the same color.

Remember President Thomas Jefferson? It is a fact that he, as well, had a family that was not the same color, and down through history, the facts were hidden until just recently someone did some research and low and behold, there they were, a whole new different family with ties to those of great prominence in this great nation.

As I researched the name in its many spellings, such as Quander, Quando, Quandoe, Quanders, Kwandoh, and Amkwando, I found them to be associated with the American Quander family that is believed to have come from Ghana to Barbados and then on to Maryland, Virginia, and the surrounding DC area, and other states as well.

As I researched further, I was more persuaded that Quander L. Wilson, Sr., was a man before his time who was born into a very historical family, and still holds, in this writer's opinion, a very prominent position in history. I cannot help but remember the look of great pride on his face when he passed this information on to me. He instructed me to hold onto this information and to pass it down to the generations of my family. He further emphasized that he wanted his grandchildren and their children and all the generations to follow, to have an account of their great heritage and that they would be able to read of him. This I have endeavored to do and will keep doing all the days of my life with the intention of sharing as much information as possible, as it is imperative to continue the history and legacy of Quander Lear Wilson, Sr.

Preacher Before His Time

Chapter 3

SPIRITUAL MAN, YET FAMILY MAN

In our time of viewing television sit-coms, we all would laugh at the actor, Bill Cosby, who played the role of a loving father who would attempt to fix things around the house. The difference between the Cosby character and Bishop Wilson was that Bishop Wilson's project would always be completed.

When I watch that show, I chuckle within myself because Dad would do some of the same things done on the show. However, if he worked on it, he stayed with it until the project was finished. I know that is where I get my tenacity from. If I start a project, I do not stop until it is finished. I learned that from him; he was always one who lived by example.

I can remember him being a great cook. Oh, those times of his spiritual fasting would produce such good food plus great cobblers of peach and apple – great meals that were fit for a king and queen, which the family consumed with great delight. During family dinner time, Bishop would sit with us and act as though he was sharing in the meal as well. Whether it was a 10, 21, or 40-day fast, he would see to it that everyone else would eat by being the chef for the duration of the fast.

Of course, there would be some humor even in the fasting phase with Bishop; there was never a dull moment. After the 40-day fast was over, Bishop would continue to cook, but this time he would join us at the table and as we would eat, you could hear Bishop say, "I wish I could eat," while all the time he would be reaching for, or asking someone to pass the rolls. Then he would follow with, "I wish I could eat," again, reaching for, or telling someone to pass the greens or pass the turkey! Oh, the times of laughter and fellowship we would have around that dining room table.

While I am on the subject of food, in the early stages of our marriage, my wife was learning how to make coffee, and at first, she would make the coffee so strong my eyelids came open by just smelling it. Every morning before I went to work, Bishop would come over to the house, and even though the coffee was very strong, and we all would make fun about it, he would say to my wife, "Rose, give me a cup of that mud." We would get a big laugh out of him drinking it and complaining about how strong it was. You would have to had been there to experience those times, to be able to fully appreciate these incidents.

Spiritual Man, Yet Family Man

Chapter 4

VISIONARY

Write the vision, and make it plain upon tables, that he may run that readeth it. Habakkuk 2:2

There will be other visionaries before the return of the Lord, but I believe there will never be one quite like Bishop Wilson. He was a man who knew the voice of the Lord and moved in the Spirit realm as well as the earthly realm to accomplish those things that were revealed to him.

He demonstrated to those who followed him that in order to have vision one had to want to walk with God and expect to hear from God. He believed there was a place in God in which you could get and the Lord would commune with you as He did with Adam in the garden. In other words, Bishop would often tell me that you had to get in the place where the Lord could talk with you and give you vision. When God communes with you, He molds and shapes you. The Lord knew if His people had no vision they would surely die, so He imparted into Bishop Wilson truths that were mind-boggling to many people.

The Lord gave Bishop Wilson "Fresh Vision" and "New Vision," which in turn caused God's people all over the world to "move with the cloud," as he said, which meant the people of God were going to another level in the Lord. A lot of spiritual things being done and talked about today were given to him many years ago. Through his teachings and examples, many went to a new place, a new level, a new direction, which in turn gave them new results.

Proverbs 29:18 says, "Where there is no vision (revelation), the people perish (cast off restraint) but he that keepeth the law, happy (blessed) is he." (New International Version) Certainly, Bishop Wilson kept the law of God in his heart. In his daily walk here on earth he took that scripture and applied it literally. He knew that vision was essential for survival, especially in the saint's walk with God. Thank God, Bishop Wilson was not selfish with what the Lord had imparted in him.

When it came to vision, one could find him developing and constantly enlarging his "Personal Vision" because he wanted to be all he could be for the Lord. Then, looking further at his example, you could find him cultivating and expanding the "Corporate Vision," because he loved the people of God and had a pressing desire for the Body of Christ in its entirety to have the best available, and enjoy life and all the things the Lord had provided for them.

Last but not least, you could see the "Spiritual Vision" that he cherished the most. It was in this that he loved to flow. He loved to talk about it – those things that the Lord had revealed to him – but he always remembered that some of those things were, as the apostle Paul said, "unlawful to utter." Therefore, he would give out bits and pieces of those things the Lord had given as he was released to share them. He would often remind us that we were the workmanship of the Lord, and that we are created in Christ Jesus to do good works. He would let us know the Lord had ordained that we should walk in them.

I learned from him and I preach often that the "Personal Vision" is the "Spiritual Vision" that the Lord gives us on a personal level, and it is up to us, as visionaries, to do as the scripture has instructed in the writings of the prophet Habakkuk in Habakkuk 2:2: "Write the vision and make it plain upon tables, that he may run that readeth it."

As I look at the life of this great man, I find that he actually built his whole ministry on the revelation that had been given to him from the Lord. By watching him, I came to the knowledge that a team carries out a vision but the team must also have a visionary. In my opinion, that means that God's people have to be led in the vision. So, God sent us a man who did all he could to stand on his watch and do those things to enhance the vision. He understood and tried to convey to us that vision was for an appointed time.

Realizing this great task, he raised up many sons and daughters to carry on the vision. He realized that the vision would not tarry, but being a man of great patience and faith, he knew and agreed that it would tarry, but it would manifest, because the scripture did declare, "It would surely come; it would not tarry." That is why he had so much faith in God; he just believed that the vision would come. He imparted as much vision and faith as he could in those who would receive it. Yes, again I say he was a man before his time.

I have found that all of us have certain qualities that we may or may not be aware of. Sometimes this causes us to doubt ourselves, but when the Lord calls you, He equips you. You may need someone to bring out the qualities that lay dormant within you. That is why everybody needs a father and mother figure, a mentor, a friend, a pastor, someone who will "keep it real" with them by telling the real truth about everything concerning them, and yet loving them all the time, and, oh yes, keeping everything confidential. Everybody needs a "truth friend."

What can be learned from the life of Bishop Wilson? We all are in a learning process. We learn from each other. As a great visionary, Bishop had an endless passion for wanting to hear from the Lord. He would get in the place where he and the Lord could commune as friend to friend. He taught me, as well as others, that you have to get in the place where the Lord can talk to you and give you strategy to go along with vision.

He was taught to be a great visionary by the awesome mentors with whom he crossed paths such as the late Bishop A. R. Jackson at the Bible Truths Center, the late Bishop Wallace W. Smith of Philadelphia, Pennsylvania, and others he met while attending and graduating from such institutions as the Philadelphia School of the Bible, the Crozier Bible Institute, and the Chester Theological Seminary, the latter two of which are located in Chester, Pennsylvania.

I believe the crowning moment of all of his learning was in 1971 when he received his Ph.D. in Theology from the Florida State Christian College in Fort Lauderdale, Florida. Being the person he was, these accomplishments never changed him or his relationship with the Lord and the people. If anything, it made him more humble.

Bishop Wilson had no problem speaking into one's life. Before the prosperity message was as popular as it is now and has been in times past, he would teach the principles of God on prosperity. Using the Bible as a guideline, he would show how God has to honor His own Word.

Another trait about him was that he always gave to those who helped him along the way. It is a wonderful thing to adopt such awesome characteristics by following Bishop's example of displaying gratitude and thanksgiving. A simple 'thank you' goes a long way. At times you may forget to thank those who have been there for you and for those who help. Just remember that what you do privately, God will reward openly.

I was present with him on occasions when he gave divinely inspired instructions to those who were standing at the crossroads of life, needing to make definite decisions, not knowing which way to go. Bishop Wilson would take time out to minister to and/or counsel those in need. It did not matter where he was or what the occasion was; he would give out what the Lord would give him concerning the individual.

I have stood with him in hospital lobbies, stood in the middle of dilapidated properties where he would tell the individuals concerned to go ahead and make the move, and that God would bless their endeavor. Those to whom he spoke would make the move. Today, many of them are going on those words and they are still being blessed.

Many are speaking the things Bishop Wilson received as a revelation years before giving it out, or before it was popular to be taught. As a matter of fact, many of them were in classes and seminars that he taught. Many went to services where he spoke and gleaned from the numerous spiritual nuggets he spoke, and now, if you listen closely, you can hear those same nuggets being spoken all over again, thus proving that they were listening when he spoke.

The phrase, "When E. F. Hutton speaks, everyone listens," has nothing on the times that Bishop Q. L. Wilson spoke and everybody listened. Now we have many great ministries, mega ministries, and even smaller ones. But if you go back to the time they started out, for some it was the words of Bishop Wilson that gave them the push they needed to get started, which in turn landed them where they are now.

To those who are still striving, don't stop now. It is those words and nuggets that have inspired you over the years and continue to even now, and give hope and encouragement to keep on keeping on. May God be glorified in it all.

I was there on so many occasions when the Spirit of the Lord would come over him, and it didn't matter where he was, or whose company he was in. He would quicken and even speak in tongues as he enjoyed the presence of the Lord.

I say as the late great newsman personality, Paul Harvey, often said, "Now you know the rest of the story."

Chapter 5

MAN OF PATIENCE

Due to our humanistic makeup, we copy from each other. If we see someone making it in life, we want to know how they did it, and if it is possible, we will copy them. But I must warn you: Everybody must strive to be themselves. One cannot be someone else, because after all the pretending, at some time or the other the real you will come out. Life itself is a schoolmaster that is constantly teaching us lessons that will remain etched in our minds forever. Some lessons that we've learned were hard lessons that took us a while to understand, and in some cases, some are still learning and have not realized even the simplest lessons.

Looking at Bishop Wilson's life, one can learn of patience and that it is a virtue. Unless you learn patience, you will be in for a rude awakening, as life will teach you to wait. Some feel as if everything they want will come in a moment and a twinkling of an eye, but not so. In this life we have to wait.

For those of us who walk with the Lord, we know we may not be able to handle life, especially the successful part, unless we are prepared for it. I believe the Lord takes us through phases in life, which in turn prepare us and get us ready for the things the Lord has in store for us.

Often in the secular world, it is known that people go through different things. They learn from the experiences they go through, and if it is a bad experience, they do all they can not to repeat that experience.

I find that in the church world, most have a problem with bad experiences. They feel as though God has forgotten them or life is so unfair, and they find themselves in a pity party and will actually invite others to join them. I learned from the life of Bishop Wilson that life holds many experiences, some good and some bad, but we learn to take the bad and use them as stepping-stones to a better life.

In the story of Job, as recorded in the Bible, we see the results and principals of patience. First of all, there has to be a genuine relationship with God, a relationship of trust and believing, that the God one serves has everything under control in spite of what is seen by the natural eye. My wife, Rose Marie, often says, "Never be moved by what you see; only be moved by the Word of God."

Job went through experiences in the natural, and just think about it, he did nothing to deserve what he went through. God, during the meeting in heaven with his sons, begin to brag about Job to Satan. As we like to say, "Job's name came up," and what God said about him to Satan immediately caused Satan to get angry. After a brief encounter and after God declared what a good man Job was, He gave Satan permission to try Job. In one sense, according to our humanistic thinking, that was good, and on the other hand, the question comes to mind, "Why Job?" The answer, "Why not Job?"

The Bible records how Job feared God and was an upright man. He would offer sacrifices for his children in order not to offend the Lord. In all of that, the carnal mind wonders why such a good man would have to suffer so much. In all of the calamities Job went through, loss of family, property, servants, and finally, the most hurtful thing a married person could hear, the harsh words of a spouse telling him to curse his God and die. He perhaps handled all of the other things that happened, even when his friends came and just sat and looked at him not saying a word. I know that many of us today would have a problem with that – someone just staring at us – especially if we were sick or having a rough time.

Another blow of disappointment came when Job's friends finally spoke to him. They were words of accusation. What an ordeal to go through! But by having patience, and trusting God, we find the conclusion of the whole matter and that was that God restored all that Job had lost.

I watched patience work through Bishop Wilson. I saw him lifted to many elevations in the Lord, and I also saw him walk through the valleys of life's disappointments. Having an outgoing personality, he reached out for people, and went to them in their time of need. However, there were times when perhaps God and Satan had a conversation and Bishop Wilson's name came up. I witnessed the times of despair, when he would say; "I have no one who understands what I am going through."

Other times I saw him physically sick, and often I would hear him ask the Lord, "Why do I have to go through this?" I have been around him when he and God would seemingly be having a down to earth conversation. I believe like the Bible says about Moses, Bishop Wilson spoke face to face with God.

In his sleep he would talk to God. When he was awakened, his natural mind could not recall anything that was said. However, by observance, one could tell he had been with the Lord. Many of us witnessed patience operating and displayed from this earthly man many times, especially during the days of fasting for 21 and 40 days. He was patient enough until it seemed as though Heaven rejoiced and hell went into convulsions because he took the time to go before the Lord of heaven and earth to get an answer on how to lead God's people and what to feed them in their time of spiritual famine.

He showed patience in dealing with people, though he seemed to be on another level spiritually than some. He showed and demonstrated great patience in waiting for God to bring them to the place where they would ultimately be.

Many were the times that he would say, "Let the Lord make them." Even when those whom he was trying to lift would turn away from him, forsake him, and say all manner of evil things, he still would show patience. Some of those who walked away did reconcile with him before he was promoted to Glory.

Looking at his life, his methods, and his convictions, one can learn a great deal about patience. Patience is something that one has to work on, cultivate, and use daily in working with God's people, and not only with God's people, but in life itself. Whether one is working in the church realm or the secular realm, it is a fact that patience is a virtue, and it is needed to sustain one in this life.

Chapter 6

MAN OF CONGENIALITY

Another thing I learned from Bishop Wilson was congeniality – how to get along with people. People are funny. In some cases, I often say, "They are a trip." Our makeup of character, our likes and dislikes, all differ. Some people can look at you and instantly not like you, while others can look at you and immediately there is a bond that occurs. We are either drawn to one another or we will distance ourselves from each other.

I find that if we will take the time that is necessary to learn each other, without getting into each other's business, but instead learn how to reason with each other and see what people are about, I believe the world would be a much better place.

The cliché, "Can't we all just get along?" does not always work. We all are different and we will have our separate but unique opinions. But when we find someone who doesn't agree with us, or looks different from us, or does things differently from how we do things, we have a tendency to keep them at arm's length. Did you ever stop and think what a boring world this would be if everybody did exactly the same thing?

Thank God we are not robots, but humans. Be honest and ask yourself this question, "Would you want the world to act and think like you act and think?" Perhaps you feel you have all the answers, but in reality, you do not, and that is why God made us so unique in our personalities, likes, and dislikes.

I observed Bishop Wilson on numerous occasions go into settings where I knew the people didn't care for him for whatever reason, but he never showed any animosity or strife. I could see the pain on his face because I knew him, but for those around him, they never knew the pain. Why? Because he allowed the Spirit of God to rest on him, and believe it or not, the Spirit of God will help you in times of despair.

I would often ask him, "How do you do it? You know they don't like you!" He would look at me and say, "Son, it's not what they think or do to me; it's about what I think and do to them." He would go on to say, "They have to give an account to the Lord for themselves; I don't have to answer for them."

I learned this from him: If you trust the Lord to deal with your enemies, the scripture will come to light that admonishes us that our enemies will become our footstool. The Spirit of God will move in such a way that those who were against you and opposed your very existence will be at peace with you because they will not be able to see what your stance or position is or even where your very fire is coming from.

I've learned not to harbor ill feelings toward anybody because when you do this, you only hurt yourself. Bishop Wilson would often say to me in a quiet, calm way, "A soft answer turneth away wrath." (Proverbs 15:1) I have found this to be a good tool for defusing the most volatile situations. I cannot say I have understood all that happened to Bishop Wilson, nor to me, but one thing I strive to do is clear the thought patterns of my mind, keep my heart pure, and try to see the good in everybody.

I will be the first to admit that sometimes it is very difficult to see the good, but if you look closely enough, you will find some good in the worst of people, and some bad in the best.

When one learns to love people, it's not hard to keep moving in life. I have seen the consequences of bitterness against people. I even attended a funeral at which the person in the casket died bitter. By the way, this person was a member of the church for years. With all the technology of today, the mortician could not erase the anger and bitterness from this person's face. Bitterness is one of those things of life that will hinder one from seeing the Lord in peace.

Oh, the things that I have learned from the most congenial man that I have ever known. Bishop taught me to be friendly to those who will allow it, and for those who do not receive me, respect their feelings, speak to them, and then shake the dust off my feet, and keep moving.

I try to do what is right, and I put into practice those things I learned from my father, the late Bishop Wilson. To sum it all up, I try to treat people the way I want to be treated. After all, that's what my Dad taught.

Chapter 7

SPIRITUAL FATHER TO MANY

For though ye have ten thousand instructors in Christ, yet have ye not many fathers: for in Christ Jesus I have begotten you through the gospel. 1 Corinthians 4:15

Bishop Wilson was a spiritual father to so many people of various backgrounds, upbringings, and spiritual persuasions. I can attest to that, as he was my spiritual father as well. Some may appear as self-made, but Bishop Wilson held the ladder for many as they climbed to the top. I was blessed to have been present in many meetings and settings in which Bishop saw something in those with whom he came in contact, and I would hear him tell them, "Go on, do what the Lord wants you to do." They would take his advice, and in a few months or years, they would be sailing high, showing the fruits of the deposit they received from the Lord through him. He was there to push you right on through to your destiny, knowing what his position was.

I can remember him pausing to impart a word of wisdom into someone's life. It did not matter where he was. On one occasion in a hospital lobby, he gave a word of instruction and encouragement to a person who was debating on launching out into ministry. Today, the person is well blessed in ministry, and I believe it was because Bishop Wilson took the role of a spiritual father and spoke into that life. He touched and changed more than one person's life.

I recall a young lady to whom he spoke the powerful words of a mentor and spiritual father. She was working to help set up another ministry within a different denomination, all the while being covered by Bishop. The time came when she had to make the decision to move from one geographical location in the country to another, placing her far away from her church and her church family, where Bishop was pastoring her. The words he spoke to her were this, "No shepherd likes to lose their sheep. It's my job to train you. It's your job to go out and do what I trained you to do." With that he bestowed upon her the apostolic blessing of a father and continued to pour into her spiritually until the day she left and beyond. To this very day, she identifies Bishop Quander L. Wilson, Sr. as her spiritual father wherever she goes, whether she is on a television show, radio, internet, or in the pulpit delivering a message.

There is something unique about those that Bishop trained or whose ministries were birthed under his tutelage. If you knew Bishop or ever heard him speak, there is a sound, a demeanor, a delivery of the Word of God, (especially in those with the gift of prophecy or word of knowledge), or something, that you can readily identify with that reminds you of such a powerful Father in the Kingdom of God. You'll find yourself saying, "hmmmm, I know this person from somewhere!" His lineage and legacy shall live throughout eternity!

By doing what he was sent on earth to do, he made the lives of so many people different in a positive way. That brings to mind the song produced and sung by the artist, Bill Withers, entitled "Lean on Me." The lyrics say, "Lean on me when you're not strong. I'll be your friend; I'll help you carry on." There are times in one's life when one needs somebody to lean on.

Bishop Wilson had the ability to see a person and look beyond what was in front of him and look into time and see great good in that person. He would take time out and pour into them those things that a true spiritual father would do. Additionally, he would deposit so much positivity, love, encouragement, and strength, that when you would leave the presence of the Lord through him, you would literally be walking on cloud nine. When you think of the wind beneath one's wings, he certainly was just that, never asking for anything in return. He was just a godly man with the true heart of a father. That brings to mind the saying, "We have many teachers, but very few fathers."

So many times, he would jump-start people with his great smile and spirit of humility, yet with a strong, firm word that would catapult them into doing whatever they wanted to do or were called into the earth realm to do.

Spiritual Father in Deeds and Actions

I see so many things that are going on now, so many preachers that are preaching from what they say is their revelation. Don't get me wrong. I know the Lord will and does inspire, but some of the things that people are going wild over now, as a young boy, I, and others as well, heard Bishop Wilson preach and teach.

At the time he was doing this, it did not make him very popular in some circles. However, he held his ground, and preached and taught. Now, there are so many sons and daughters that have benefited from those teachings that showed them how to survive, and not only how to survive, but how to live life to its fullest.

This type of teaching can only come from divine revelation; you don't readily gain it from books. It comes from spending time with the Lord, which I saw Bishop do on a daily basis. You could be riding in a car, thinking he was talking to you, and before you knew it, there was that heavenly language being sounded in your ears, and often you would see a hand go up. Other times, tears would stream down his cheeks as he did what Moses did in the Bible. It seemed like Bishop Wilson would go to the mountain top and the Lord would come down and meet him and they would commune as friend to friend, like Moses.

Many times, when we would travel, you could rest assured that by the time you got to your destination, you would have learned or received a course in the area of kingdom living, kingdom mentality, and kingdom authority, as only a spiritual father could impart.

If it were possible, the highways between Ohio, Pennsylvania, and Maryland would give out some valuable lessons of faith, as this was what Bishop Wilson did as he drove the bus over the road, taking the saints to and from the Holy Convocation in Portsmouth, Ohio. Now, think about it, what Chief Apostle that you know, other than one who sits in the seat of a spiritual father, would drive a bus from state to state and make sure the people of God who wanted to attend would have transportation to such an event. Sounds like a father looking out for his children to me.

It was during those trips that we would receive the same teachings that are offered by many authors and preachers of today. This divine revelation was on time then and it is still on time now for the people of today. Whether we were in a car or a bus, and in the later years, on an airplane or just sitting around the kitchen table, in the living room or even in a restaurant enjoying a good meal, words cannot describe the depth of refreshing inspiration we received from Bishop Wilson, our spiritual father.

There was an occasion in which this divine revelation came to the forefront. A pastor whom Bishop considered as one of his spiritual sons, was facing serious surgery. Because of divine revelation, Bishop sensed fear in his voice as they discussed the ordeal. Bishop prayed for him over the phone, and the next thing we knew, Bishop was on the highway, making his way to the hospital. He stood by the bedside of the one who was to have the surgery, and when the question was asked of Bishop, "Why did you come? You didn't have to come!" Bishop's answer was, "I came to see about you, because I heard fear in your voice." I believe through the prayer of Bishop, that person did not have the scheduled operation because of the healing power of God through prayer. We can say for a surety Bishop Wilson had the heart of a spiritual father, which we are hard pressed to find in today's society. Again, the scripture comes to life:

For though ye have ten thousand instructors in Christ, yet have ye not many fathers: for in Christ Jesus I have begotten you through the gospel. 1 Corinthians 4:15

What a man of God he was. He could listen to you and diagnose what he heard you saying, and then act on it. I remember his preaching and teaching in the church, especially during the Holy Convocations in the early morning sessions, but he could take you to Bible study any time and any place. He always had a word that he could impart into the life of anyone who would take the time to listen to what he had to say. He would impart a spiritual seed into you that would quicken your spiritual desires and awaken those gifts that were lying dormant in you from the beginning of your life. He would release certain blessings on you because he had the spirit of a spiritual father.

It is sad, but real spiritual fathers are hard to find. That's why when you find a true spiritual father, hold on to him, reverence him, and bless him as much as possible. Don't worship him, for we worship God, but hold him in high esteem. In doing so, make sure you give and receive all that God has for you in that relationship. I'll reference here a favorite cliché I often quote: "Learn all you can and can all you learn," as it will be a blessing to you down through your life.

I can remember the day he declared he would tear-up his mantle and impart a piece of it to all of his spiritual sons and daughters. Today I feel so blessed, because I have a lot of spiritual brothers and sisters all over not just the United States, but the world, who have a piece of my dad's mantle. I dare say, there are those who have some of his characteristics in their teachings, preaching, and mannerisms. This is understood because when you have the blessing of a spiritual father you certainly will have his characteristics.

Chapter 8

MAN OF HUMILITY AND COMPASSION

What I am about to share here may ruffle a few feathers but remember as I stated in the beginning of my writings. Nothing said is meant to offend or harm anyone. What I speak is my truth.

So many times, Bishop's humility was mistaken for weakness. I have even heard it said that his compassion was mistaken for something else other than what it was. The rumors that the organization he founded, Greater Emmanuel International Fellowship of Churches and Ministries, Inc., was riddled with adverse people with adverse ideas have been circulated far and near. As I am one of the original members of the Greater Emmanuel Fellowship, I can say with complete conviction, my father taught the Word of God.

Any time you have a gathering of people, you are going to get just what the Bible speaks of in the vision that the Apostle Peter had concerning the great net that was cast down and came up with all kinds of animals. There were a lot of people who perhaps should have been "turned out" according to the rules of man, but Bishop Wilson practiced what the Word of God said: "Brethren, if a man be overtaken in a fault, ye which are spiritual, restore such a one in the spirit of meekness; considering thyself, lest thou also be tempted." (Galatians 6:1)

The church does not do much restoring in this day and time. It is what we should be doing, but instead, many stand afar off and have become professional finger pointers. Had there not been compassion and understanding displayed by Bishop Wilson, and had they not been restored spiritually, a lot of people would not be in the positions they are in now. Perhaps they would not even be the leaders they are today. One of the things I have come to understand is summed up in a cliché I heard in my youth spoken by the older saints: "A heap see, but a few know."

I know of those who called him inept but he kept on loving them. When they really should have been dismissed, he kept pouring into them, and they survived. There were private and not so private meetings held, full of contempt and conspiracy. But he still maintained his posture of integrity and dignity and never lost his cool.

He kept displaying humility and compassion towards all manner of men (and women), which made him a man among men, and the man before his time. Many would have lost it, probably thrown in the towel, perhaps let their emotions run away with them, and perhaps given them a piece of their mind, but he always would say to me when I was ready to go off because of what was happening, "Don't give a piece of your mind to people because sooner or later, you won't have any mind left."

His humility and compassion are felt as we read the poem he composed while in service at "Azusa '93" in Tulsa, Oklahoma, entitled, "That's My Purpose." In this beautiful poem he pours out the sentiments of his heart, saying what he didn't mind doing in order for others to make it to the top.

He spoke of being many things – a cleaning mop, and a band that held families together. Then he spoke of the standards of men, which, in their sight, he admitted, they saw him as a "fool." He stated in his poem, when his work on earth was finished, he would shout loudly in glory, his purpose being fulfilled, and knowing he had done what he was supposed to do. I believe when he gets to glory, he will remind the angels more than once, telling them, "I did what I was supposed to do."

The poem has been shared in the chapter entitled, "Pappy."

Chapter 9

APOSTLE AMONG APOSTLES

Bishop Wilson with Pastor Ron West, Bishop David Daniels, Jr.

A servant of Jesus Christ, called to be an apostle, separated unto the gospel of God. Romans 1:1

I have been around the church and church people just about all my life, so you can imagine the things I have heard and seen. In today's church world, I have heard and read the various comments concerning the office of the apostle in the 21st century church.

Some people in these times change their titles on their own without an apostolic anointing or appointment from

God. One time you see them they may be an evangelist, pastor, preacher, etc. The next time you see them, they will have changed their title to apostle. I remember at one time in the Christian arena, the going title was that of a bishop.

I recall being in a meeting of bishops and elders in one of our fellowship call meetings in which a statement was made concerning the office and title of a bishop. The person, who was already a bishop, said, "You can buy bishops a dime a dozen."

Having just been consecrated to the office of bishop, that statement hurt. I made it up in my mind at that time, regardless of how many people view or carry the title of bishop, I would take to heart the office that I serve. I vowed to do all I could to make the office of bishop one of dignity to the best of my ability, as well as endeavor, as I have to this day, to try to be the best of the best when it comes to being a bishop.

I have seen some who were elevated to the office of bishop have personal problems, but that does not keep me from holding to my determination and desire, that is, being one of the best preachers ever consecrated to the office. My plan is to do as it is recorded in Habakkuk 2:1. "I will stand upon my watch, and set me upon the tower, and will watch to see what he will say unto me and what I shall answer when I am reproved."

When it comes to the office of an apostle, that seems to be the going title for now. It's all good in the secular world, for as I often heard the late Apostle Quander L. Wilson, Sr. say, "Make your call and election sure." There is much talk as to whether there are any apostles in this day and time. I believe the office of the apostle still stands today as it did in biblical times.

It is a known fact that the apostles of today are not the same as the apostles were during the time of Jesus. We all know the apostles of today did not see or walk with the Lord Jesus Christ physically as some of those of the Bible. However, I believe there are genuine apostles in this day and time who are ordained by the Lord, and in turn, are commissioned by their peers to work in the church of today, which we call the 21st century church.

For a moment, let's examine some of the scriptures that deal with the apostle and the office of the apostle. In Ephesians 2:19 & 20, the apostle Paul lets the saints of that day and also the saints of today know that "We are fellow-citizens with the saints, and of the household of God and are built upon the foundation of the apostles and prophets with Jesus Christ himself being the chief corner stone."

By reading that passage we understand that we, the church of today, are built upon the foundation that the apostles laid. Certainly, we can say that Bishop Wilson laid a foundation upon which quite a few people have built. Even unto this day, they are building upon it.

In Ephesians 4:11 we find the apostle Paul writing again, saying, "And he gave some apostles, and some prophets, and some evangelists, and some pastors and teachers." In verse 12, the apostle Paul shared why these positions were given, with the apostle being named first. He stated they were for the "perfecting of the saints, for the work of the ministry, for the edifying of the body of Christ."

That verse alone lets us, as believers, know that in the New Testament Church there would be apostles to help perfect the church. If there was ever a person who wanted to help perfect the church, that person was Bishop Quander L. Wilson, Sr.

As we read about apostles, we see that the apostles showed signs, which confirmed and made them apostles. Apostle Paul said the signs of an apostle were wrought among the people as he, Apostle Paul, showed patience, signs, wonders, and mighty deeds. (Read 2 Corinthians 12:12).

Apostle Paul also said he took pleasure in infirmities, reproaches, necessities, persecutions, and distresses for Christ's sake, and right after that he said that he became a fool in glorying. Then he tells the people, church people, "you should have compelled me, for I ought to have been commended of you, for in nothing am I behind the very chiefest apostles, though I be nothing."

As one looks at the life of the late Bishop Wilson, we find that he bore the signs of an apostle. He was truly a man of patience and humility. Everywhere he went and whomever he ministered to he left a positive sign. Those with whom he had contact were delivered and encouraged. Many who knew him wondered how he was able to bridge the gap between the generations and races. Yes, through all of that, you could say he did mighty deeds as an apostle.

I saw him on many occasions lay his hands on people. The Holy Ghost would move on and through him, and many would be set free from ailments and entrapments of the adversary.

I even saw him pray and then speak to the weather and ask God to clear up the storm, and it happened. The storm ceased and fair weather prevailed.

Afterward, Bishop reminded me of the words of Christ, as found in His discourse to the disciples, after He had cursed the fig tree for not producing fruit. "And all things, whatsoever ye shall ask in prayer, believing, ye shall receive." (Matthew 21:22)

Bishop Wilson, like the apostle Paul, took pleasure in life's infirmities, reproaches, necessities, and even in persecutions and distresses for Christ's sake, the churches' sake. He held on, as Job did, to his integrity, and would often tell me, "In all things give thanks." He made me to understand that he was not giving thanks for the things he was going through but he was giving thanks while he was in whatever he was going through for he knew the Lord would bring him out.

So, I believe that Bishop Wilson was one of the 21st century apostles. Because of the dunamis power of God working in and through him, he was able to preach, and operate in the gift of healing, eliminating and eradicating sicknesses by allowing the anointing of God to work through him. I witnessed the mighty works of God working through him on many occasions during his many revivals.

Demonic Encounters

I also saw the delivering works of God work through him in casting out evil spirits. It was during those times that I learned about demonic spirits and how to cast them out. He would often tell me, "I don't go looking for demonic spirits, but when I encounter one, I know what to do, and so should you."

One thing you could say concerning Bishop Wilson is that he would share with you and teach you if you wanted to be taught. I can remember having to use what he had told me. On one occasion during one of his 40-day fasts, I was on my way to work. Bishop would always be in his morning prayer around the time I would leave. On this particular day, as I approached my car, I could hear my father travailing before the Lord. It sounded like he had encountered a demonic spirit because I could hear him rebuking and coming against an evil spirit. Well, to my surprise, as I approached a space between his house and my house, I saw the most hideous, demonic spirit I had ever seen. It was huge in statue, ugly in appearance, and black in color. It looked at me and faded away right before my eyes. I will be honest with you and tell you I was startled and scared, but I used what I had been taught to do when confronted by a demonic spirit. I pleaded the blood of Jesus. As fast as this demonic spirit appeared outside of the wall of the house, it disappeared.

Shaken, I made my way to my father and told him of the encounter. He informed me that he indeed had had an encounter with and had to rebuke the same demonic spirit because it confronted him, offering him various things as the devil did when he confronted Christ after Christ had been on His 40-day fast.

Yes, demons are for real, and I thank God to this day for the advice that my father gave me. To this day, I have no problem pleading the blood of Jesus on anything, anybody, and in any situation. I have been criticized for doing this by so called church folk, of all people, but I believe, and I know there is power in the blood.

Should you ever get in trouble, should you ever be attacked by a demonic force, take my advice: Plead the blood of Jesus. It worked for me then, and it still works for me today. I am sure it will do the same for you.

The Word of God as a Tool

To back up what Bishop Wilson taught, he would always have a Bible somewhere close. Of course, in my opinion, he did not need the Bible that much, for he was well versed in the Word of God.

So many times when I would be putting a sermon together, I would call him and he would give me the scripture, the meaning of the scripture, and anything else that was important to the sermon. He never gave the impression that he knew it all; he just kept a Bible handy, by his bedside, in the car, wherever he was. He would often tell me, "No workman goes out without his tools," and I believe this to be true. This is where I learned to always have a Bible near me. Even in my secular job, I make sure I have my tool, the Bible, with me.

Bishop was a true apostle. You could see the apostleship upon him as it was on those in the days of old. He had the outspokenness or the boldness and plainness of speech. He spoke openly and freely and with confidence when sharing the Word of God.

He was one who was not destitute of knowledge about the Lord. He was blessed to have divine knowledge, which I believed came from the throne of the Lord.

When you understand the manner in which one becomes an apostle, you will find there is a process. Note the qualifications for the office of an apostle. I believe there are five qualities that should be present for one seeking this office. Note them if you will:

1. I believe an apostle must have the heart of a spiritual father.

2. I believe an apostle must have a deep love for and loyalty to the church of God.

3. I believe an apostle has to be accountable to a pastor who in turn is responsible for him.

4. I believe an apostle must show and demonstrate patience, and not be given to self-glory.

5. I believe if one wants to be an apostle, he must have a servant's heart.

My father, along with the Holy Ghost, taught me something called patience. This is one of the particularly important characteristics that an apostle must have. Not only does the Lord have to ordain the elevation within the individual, but the Spirit of the Lord will move on one's peers, and they will be inspired by the Holy Ghost to see the works, accomplishments, and spirituality of the one called to the office of the apostle.

I believe at a specified time the one designated will be called out and hands laid upon him as a candidate for the office. While the candidate is waiting with patience for the confirmation, the Holy Ghost will further prepare him to receive the position for which he has been called.

Chapter 10

PASTOR AMONG PASTORS

*And I will give you pastors according to mine heart, which
shall feed you with knowledge and understanding..."*
Jeremiah 3:15

In the writings of the prophet Jeremiah (Jeremiah 3:14 & 15) we find the words of the Lord telling Israel to turn because He, God, was married to them, and He would take one of a city, and two of a family, bring them to Zion, and give to them pastors according to his heart, who would feed them with knowledge and understanding.

I would dare say that Bishop Wilson was a pastor among pastors. He was a man who had so many qualities of a true pastor. Bishop Wilson was a "man after God's own heart" who fed the flock with divine knowledge and understanding. He knew God and taught the law of God, and lived free from sin as much as humanly possible. He turned down many lucrative offers and sought after those things that were really profitable to him in the spiritual realm.

As a pastor, he was sensitive and reasonable to those who sought the Lord. He showed he was willing to lay down his natural life for those who were in the vineyard of the Lord and needed protection. He went beyond his duty and gathered the lost sheep, comforting them in their fearful, stressful times. So many would not be pastors today had it not been for the wise counsel of Bishop Wilson. Growing up in his household, it was nothing for him to leave out in the early morning hours or spend late hours with a pastor who had lost hope or was going through something with their congregation.

I saw him stand as a buffer between a warring pastor and his congregation. When some pastors made elementary mistakes, and did it more than once, Bishop Wilson was only a phone call away. What I liked about it was that he would give correction where correction was needed, and inspiration when the pastor, as well as the congregation, was uninspired. He taught various pastors how to be pastors even when their services were not wanted. I for one often thanked him for his kind words of wisdom and correction in my initial years and my years of being a pastor.

I believe the reason Bishop Wilson had a wealth of knowledge within was that he sought after God and spent time with Him, thus learning the ways of God, receiving the council of God, and in turn imparting what the Lord had given to him into those who would receive it. By doing that, he caused men, women, boys, and girls to change from their negative ways. He spoke God's Word faithfully, causing so many people to not only remember God, but to remember the many promises that were spoken in God's Word.

In the writings of the apostle Paul in Ephesians 4:11, we see that the gift of pastors is one of those precious gifts given to the church for the perfecting of the saints. Instead of doing as others who said they were pastors did, looking for the many imperfections and failures found in those who walked with the Lord, Bishop would do as the Lord did. He looked beyond their faults and did all he could to bring the saints to a level in the Lord where the standards of holiness were seen in a different light. He taught people about the fullness of the standards of God and how they could be put into practice right here on earth. Yes, he was a pastor among pastors.

Chapter 12

FATHER OF FATHERS

I would like to share with you the blessing of having a father of fathers. As you may or may not know, this writer was adopted by Bishop Wilson at what may be considered an early age to some. To others, I was an old adoptee, being 14 years old when Bishop and Mother Wilson adopted me, making me a member of the Wilson family. From that age,

I entered into a life-changing experience that taught me so many wonderful things, and today I feel those experiences have brought me thus far.

Dad had so much love and empathy for people; even with those who did not care for him or like him. He always showed respect, love, and compassion. I watched him go into meetings where I knew things were not in his best interest, but with a smile, and the love of God in his heart, he would go in, sit down, enjoy the service, and leave out.

There were times I would get angry within myself after finding out that others had done him wrong. When I thought he should have fought back, because of the hurt and pain caused, he would tell me, "That's not my nature." Now don't get the idea that Pappy never got angry, for there were times when he would get fed up, and as a father, he would get on me and my late brother, Larry. I remember those times when a vein would stand out in the middle of his forehead, and when you saw that, well, some of you who knew him, you know the rest of the story.

Allow me to deal with the role of a father. When one speaks of being a father, it means more than just bringing a child into the world. I have heard so many times, "Anybody can be a father, but it takes a man to be a daddy." I see it the other way around. Anybody can be a daddy, but it takes a man to be a father. As fathers we are admonished not to provoke our children to wrath but to bring them up in the nurture (child training) and admonition (warning, reproof) of the Lord, as expressed in Ephesians 6:4.

In Colossians 3:21, fathers are admonished again in bringing up children. The apostle Paul tells fathers to "provoke not your children to anger, lest they be discouraged" or in other words, have their spirit broken.

Another biblical truth that is spoken in this day and time is that there are a lot of teachers but very few fathers. There are many men who have produced children have failed in their duties as a father for whatever reason, and there are a multitude of reasons.

However, the Bible gives us instructions on bringing up our children. I never believed that it was God's will for a mother to struggle to raise a family alone. I know and understand events in life may cause families to become a one-parent family, and my respect, prayers, and support, go out to those who have had to raise, and are raising a family alone. I know when people find themselves in that position, it takes the Lord Almighty to help them to raise their family, but I have seen some incredibly positive results come from a one-parent family.

You will most likely agree with me when I say we have a generation here now that is angry, discouraged, broken-spirited, hurting, and unloved, all because of the lack of having a father. These things come back to haunt those who have fathered children, enjoyed the process of bringing a life into the world, but somehow seem to forget the rest of the story and walk off, leaving the mother, in most cases, to care for and be both the mother and father. That child, whether it be male or female, is left without love, instructions, or a role model from the father.

It seems as if this generation has been left to raise themselves, which is totally against what the Bible instructs. I can say of a truth that Bishop Wilson was a father of fathers. He showed by example what it was to be a father. I try to emulate what I saw him do for me by doing all I can for my family.

As much as I love and appreciate my adoptive parents in the person of Quander and Mary Wilson, I know that Dad was not just a father to me, but to so many others. I'm certain that you who are reading this could very well recall an incident or situation where Dad stepped in and helped you out, just as any good father would do.

There are so many accounts that I surely can't list them all. However, there was one young lady who needed tires on her car and didn't have the money to purchase them. Dad paid for the tires with the young lady vowing to pay him back and that she did, with a check. Unfortunately, the check bounced and when it did, she promised to pay him back once again. With the love and compassion of a father, he simply tore the check into pieces and deposited it into the trash, refusing to allow her to give him one dime of the money that was owed to him.

On other occasions, there were those who literally took advantage of him and things that belonged to him came up missing, with him knowing full well that he hadn't misplaced them. Instead of prosecuting them, he covered them and prayed for them because he didn't want any of his children to be in trouble with the law.

Now don't get me wrong, he was no pushover. When you needed to be scolded, he did so, but he did it with love and kindness, just like our heavenly father would have done.

He housed many and provided shelter, food, clothing, and counsel for those who needed it and had no other source or resource to turn to. Over and over again, he was a father to those inside and outside of the church. He had a way of communicating with everyone while garnering the respect that was due him, not only as a man of God, but as a Godly father.

Father of Fathers

Chapter 13

ANOINTED MAN

The Shepherd watching over the flock

This great man, Bishop Wilson, did experience the apostolic anointing of God. I often wonder, as he's been promoted to Glory, if those of my era, and the era to come, will experience and use the apostolic anointing in their daily lives, such as he did. God still has an abundance of that same powerful, life changing anointing that he bestowed upon Bishop and other men of that era and it is still available for us today.

He was one of a few men of God that I observed operating in all of the gifts spoken of in Ephesians 4:11. We referred to them as the five-fold ministry gifts. Apostle, prophet, evangelist, pastor, and teacher; select any one of those and if you were in attendance at any service in which he was either ministering or even in the audience as an attendee, you would experience at least one, if not all, of those gifts. When the Holy Spirit would move, He would use Bishop Wilson to the fullest degree. In that day, you would see healing, deliverance, and salvation take place! On the spot!

Sometimes you would experience what I call a boomerang effect. A word of healing would be spoken by the Lord through Bishop and not just one person but multitudes would be healed and the manifestation of the gifts would be seen immediately! When the spirit of salvation was in operation, you would see throngs of souls on the altars receiving the precious gift of the Holy Ghost, with the evidence of speaking in other tongues, as on the day of Pentecost!

An Anointed Teacher and Apostle

There are times that I still get frustrated concerning life, but as Bishop Wilson would often tell me in the words of an old song the saints used to sing, "Further along, we'll know all about it, further along we'll understand why." He would go on to say, "In the meantime, walk in the sunshine, for we'll understand it better by and by." Those things he taught me during those powerful one-on-one encounters with him and the Lord are markers in my learning about the anointing of God through the Apostle Quander L. Wilson. It is the anointing that destroys yokes of bondage! It is the anointing that opens some doors and closes other doors. Have you ever experienced someone, perhaps even a stranger, just bless you for no reason? It's the anointing of God on your life! The anointing draws good and bad to you. Believe me, because of it, sometimes folk will attempt to do you in, but it's the anointing of God that can protect you and not allow harm or danger to come to you! These are things that I learned through the anointing that I observed on the life of the man of God, Apostle Quander L. Wilson.

My Personal Experience

I once had a conversation with the Holy Spirit, and in my complaint, I was telling all of the things that I was going through. I reminded the Lord of how I had sacrificed so much of my life by not indulging and engaging in secular things, and I even reminded the Lord that others who were not as dedicated nor as loyal as I seemingly were getting over in life.

The Lord stopped me in my conversation, and I heard the voice of the Lord say, "You chose the anointing." You can figure out what happened from that point on. I simply stopped my complaining and went about my business.

Oh, those times of him pouring into my life have helped me maintain in the good times and the bad times. I found out it was the anointing of the Lord that has kept me going even to this day.

The State of the Church Today

Unfortunately, because of ignorance of the operation of the apostolic anointing, and people not really understanding what it means, many have been driven away from the church by some taking the apostolic anointing and making a doctrine out of it. However, I believe the apostolic anointing is for everybody, and because of what I believe, I am known to share that I am Pentecostal in experience and Apostolic in doctrine. As a child of God, I have the same rights and privileges that the apostles had. I can expect to experience the mighty moves of the Spirit as they did by invoking the apostolic anointing.

I am confident that the saints of old, as well as Bishop Wilson, did not have all the answers, and certainly there were mistakes made, but who will step in and take their place? In our churches of today, we have come a long way from the way things were when I was a young man. Our churches are fine, furniture is plush, praise teams have almost replaced the choir, musicians do not donate their talents but demand a salary (in some cases, the musician receives the salary while the pastor goes lacking). You will find various ministries have come forth and have helped many, but I find with all of these blessings, there seems to be is a lack of hunger and thirstiness for the apostolic anointing, as well as lack of commitment.

I have seen spiritual babes trying to be birthed in the church, but there was not enough power to bring them through. Oh, that we would all strive to become closer and closer to God, as Bishop Wilson did in his lifetime, and experience the apostolic anointing.

I have heard many say that church is not like it used to be. I conclude that the church as we knew it basically is no longer. The reason is that generation of saints who brought us along is just about gone. However, we have the opportunity to and must utilize that same word, same power, and that same anointing to bring back what we believe has been lost and we will experience the awesome miracle, signs, and wonders of old.

Church can be like it once was if we all would do the things that those saints did. If we would have the same dedication and tenacity, and fast and pray as they did, I believe we would see a move of God such as never seen before. After all, we are to do greater things in the Lord than our fore-parents did. Who knows, with all the knowledge that the generations have in this day and time, we may find some way to get the church going like it used to be. We can allow and encourage this generation to use all of their technologically empowered knowledge to bring us into the 21st century while making it appealing to them and invoking the anointing of God in their lives, and yet see God move as He desires to do so.

Chapter 14

"PAPPY"

In this chapter, I want to share some things I saw in Bishop Wilson that makes me think he was a man before his time. I will often refer to him as "Pappy," a nickname that was given to him many years ago. He was so down to earth that you could call him Pappy and he would just smile and receive the enduring greeting, even though he may not have known you. As time went on, those who knew him would forget and even in church would refer to him as Pappy.

I remember on one occasion a politician who was running for public office stopped by the church where one of our meetings was being held. After he had made his brief speech, he turned to Bishop Wilson, and said, "I hear so many people call you Pappy. I just want to be one of those who can call you Pappy also." That was the type of person Pappy was, it did not make any difference whether you knew him or not; he would win you over with his personality.

As I started to compare him to a few of the characters in the Bible, I would often tease him and call him by their name. For instance, as I read the story of Moses, there were glimpses of Moses' and Pappy's lives going along the same track. Moses' sister was able to be with him and help raise him, and when I look at Pappy's life, he too had a sister who was very close to him. When he and Aunt Hattie Roberts of Philadelphia, Pennsylvania, got together, it was a fun time. Sometimes I thought they were having a contest on who could speak in tongues the most. They really loved each other.

They both had a hunger and thirst for the Lord, and they were immensely powerful in their relationship with the Lord. I know this for a fact. On one occasion, one winter day, I fell on some ice while getting out of a car. Aunt

Hattie and Pappy saw me when I fell. I thought for sure I had broken my arm. I was having some serious pain. My arm was swelling up, and the first thing I thought about was to go to the hospital, but the two of them said, "Let's pray," and they both laid their hands on my arm. Before I knew it, the pain was gone, and I did not have to go to the hospital. Now you may say that was just a coincidence, but according to what I have been taught and what the scriptures say, "The prayers of the righteous availeth much."

Pappy was one who put others before himself. I examined the following poem that he was inspired to write during his time of fellowship in Tulsa, Oklahoma, during Azusa '93. It was there and in this poem that I believe the inner man of Pappy spoke the sentiments of his heart.

<u>My Purpose</u>

If I can be a road that leads someone else to fame,
If I can be the billow that fans their dying flame,
If I can hold the ladder for someone else to climb,
and help dispel the darkness and cause the light to shine,
If I can be a tunnel to bring somebody through
To finally reach and accomplish the things
That God would have them do,

Thank God, I will have done what it was meant for me to do.

"Pappy"

If I can be the band that holds some family together,
If I can be the umbrella that shelters someone from the
stormy weather,
If I can be the healing oil in someone's open wound,
Or help someone stumbling in the darkness to reach the
light of their day at noon,
If I have to go to the bottom to bring someone else to
the top,
Or clean up someone's mess of life by being the cleaning
mop,

That's my purpose! Thank God, I will have done what it
was meant for me to do.

If I have to stay in the background to push another to the
front,
Or do a deed that must be done when the one who should
do it won't,
If I can tell the faint in heart to keep on keeping on,
And let them know that the darkest hour is just before the
dawn,
If I can be the hidden force and let another take the glory,
And let them take the things I've said and the things I've
done, yet not be envious when they tell it as their own
story,
I know when I do things like this it's not according to the
rule
Because by some men's standard I'm nothing but a fool.
But when my work on earth is finished, and my course of
life is through,

I will shout this loudly in glory:
My Purpose is fulfilled; I have done what I was supposed
to do!

As you read this poem, you can feel the words come to life. He let it be known that he didn't mind being the road that leads someone else to fame. He stayed in the background and shoved others so many times. He didn't mind fanning others' dying flame or being the ladder holder for someone else to climb. With his warm smile, he turned so many dark places in people's lives to light. I find very few people are willing to be a conduit to bring somebody through to their destiny and accomplishments, but he realized that his purpose in life was to help others and that is what he did.

There are many who found Pappy to be an umbrella that sheltered them in their time of storms. He always knew how to pour in the oil and wine to heal the open wounds of those who would come to him bleeding from life's many pitfalls and circumstances. He was one who did not mind balancing stumbling people as they made their way in life. He would always manage to help them reach the light at the end of their tunnel.

He often went to the bottom of life's horrible pit to rescue and bring to the top those who were entrapped. He didn't mind getting his hands dirty to clean up somebody else's mess in life. He, on more than one occasion, became the cleaning mop as well as the floor mat because he knew what his purpose was. I am sure that at some time, he and the Lord had a conversation on the matter, and he was told what his role would be in the lives of others.

In the years I knew him, I saw him doing deeds that others were supposed to do and did not and would not do. He pushed others to the front so many times and remained in the background, telling the faint of heart to keep on keeping on, and telling them that the darkest hour was just before the dawn of their day. We, and all that knew him, must admit that he was the hidden force that let us take the glory while he never fought for himself. He didn't get envious, jealous, or angry when others took the credit for things he had done or spoke things that he had spoken as if they were their own.

Pappy was a man among men because he didn't act according to the rules laid down by man. He knew by society's rules and men's standards he seemed to be a fool, but he always believed that the Lord was keeping a record of his deeds done here on earth. So, he went to Glory believing that when his work here on earth was finished, and his course of life was through, he would wake up in Glory and shout loudly that his purpose had been fulfilled on earth and that for a surety, he had done what he was supposed to do while here with his colleagues.

Pappy the Evangelist

There has been the comparison of Pappy to the great King David. As David started out as a mere shepherd boy, and stepped onto the scene out of nowhere and slew the giant, Goliath, which brought him great fame, Pappy came out of seemingly nowhere, and began to kill many Goliath's in so many people's lives by taking the Word of God and preaching the freedom found in that Word to the people of God. Just as the Lord raised up Jonathan to be a friend to David, Pappy had a friend also, a mighty man of God, the late Bishop Wallace W. Smith, who also shared with me the times and adventures of the two of them.

When I read more of the story of Moses, I found that Moses went through a lot of circumstances before he became the great leader, as did Pappy. He would often tell me of being on the road, going to preach somewhere with Bishop Smith. One time, the car broke down and Pappy had to crawl under it and fix it and go on to preach. When they got to where they were to preach, the offerings were so low that they had to rely on the Lord to make a way for them to get to the next meeting.

He once told me of receiving a buffalo nickel as the total offering for that evening. He also told me that the people for whom they were running the revival told them breakfast would be prepared for them the next day, and sure enough, on the next day, he and Bishop Smith had two dried out wieners for breakfast. What an insult of insults for the "Dynamic Duo" as they were called; two great men of God. At the time of most of their journeys, they gained much acclaim by their preaching and music playing, along with singing. The Batman and Robin of today had nothing on the Dynamic Duo of that day.

EVANGELISTIC DUO

Rev. W. W. SMITH   Rev. Q. L. WILSON

As I listened to those incidents, I knew within my heart it would take a mighty burning bush for this preacher to become a traveling evangelist who stayed on the road like that team did, although sometimes I occasionally go out and evangelize. From what I heard and have learned about being on the field of evangelizing, it takes an incredibly special person to be an evangelist.

But again, as we grew to know Pappy, he was an evangelist among evangelists. God groomed Pappy for greatness. He may not have been in the desert in a literal sense, but for a while, it seemed as if he was obscured from everybody. Finally, the time was right. I always remind those who want to go out and start up ministries or go on the field of evangelism, they must have God's timing and blessing in order for what is started to be blessed. When the Lord was ready for Pappy to lead His people from bondage, God sent the word to him by the late Mother Gertrude Boyd of Charleston, West Virginia, with the message that the Lord had given her. It was to tell him to gather His people together, and this was what he did.

Today, so many have a testimony of victory that because of Pappy, they are enjoying their spiritual freedom. I watched as different organizations and fellowships would call for him to speak and he would say they would bring out the best in him.

He often said that all people need to hear the gospel. He taught me as well as others that you can go anywhere and just preach the gospel, not doctrine, and the Lord will come in and bless your words. I found this to be true, as he instilled in me, "Go when you are called on, preach the Word, and when the Lord gets through speaking, sit down and shut up."

I still practice this in my ministry today, and I have passed it on to those who are under my leadership. When the Lord is through, I'm through. I still carry a note that he passed to me one Sunday morning before I stood to minister. It instructed me to "Preach the Word" along with some other instructions. I read it before I minister and it is still powerful for today.

A Comparison to Biblical Characters

Like King David, Pappy desired to build a house for the Lord. Unlike David, the Lord allowed Pappy to build a new house for the Lord in a northern Ohio town called Oberlin. In my opinion, that building still stands today as a memorial to his works here on earth. I believe it can be said of Pappy as it was said of David, that he was a man after God's own heart.

I often compared Pappy to Job, for Pappy feared God, as did Job, and avoided evil as much as humanly possible. I must say this, no one on the topside of the earth is perfect. I heard this cliché as a young boy: "There is some good in the worst of us, and some bad in the best of us." With that being said, I don't know of anything in Bishop Wilson's life that was bad. I am sure he had his issues, as it is human nature in all of us.

There is always something said about a person after they are gone and not able to respond to allegations.

Whatever anyone has heard about this man, whether it be good or bad, rest assured, we all will stand before a righteous God and give an account of the deeds done in this body, whether they be good or bad.

When people read about Job, they think that Job was perfect as pertaining to being without sin or not having any tendencies to do evil, but as you know, until this old mortal has put on immortality, we all have to fight what seemingly tries to overtake us.

When you research the word "perfect" in the sense that it is used in the scripture concerning Job, it means that Job was a human being that was upright among the people or his peers, kind to his family, just to his neighbors, and benevolent to those who were less fortunate then he was. Pappy was the same way. He was free from any evil intentions toward anyone, he loved the Lord with all of his heart, and Pappy would often tell you, "I'm human. Be patient with me; God is not through with me yet." In the waning days of his life, he let me know that he felt he had not accomplished much, but I assured him that although there were no great monuments of brick and mortar in his honor, and though it seemed as if those whom he had helped and encouraged were nowhere to be found, God was aware of all of it. I would often tell him to be encouraged when he was down. I am sure he felt somewhat like

Nehemiah. Notice the last verse of Nehemiah's writings: "Remember me, O my God for good."

Nehemiah had a strong passion for the things of God, and desired to rebuild the walls and the city of Jerusalem. As Nehemiah's efforts were to do what was right for the Lord, I believe the Lord remembers Pappy for "the good" as we who knew him remember. As I read the account of Nehemiah, I could see a lot of Pappy in him.

The adversary came to hinder the work of the Lord. Nehemiah was able to get things done; it wasn't easy, but he did it. I saw the many hindrances Pappy encountered as he endeavored to do the will of God.

Nehemiah had three adversaries to deal with – Sanballat, Tobiah, and Geshem – who tried their best to get Nehemiah to come down off the wall and waste time with them. Nehemiah ended up telling them that he was doing a great work and could not come down and questioned them as to why he should stop and come down.

As Pappy went about rebuilding the spiritual Jerusalem, there were many who wanted him to come down from the wall and waste time with them, but as always, he was able to out-think, out-pray, and out-maneuver the Sanballets, Tobiahs, and the Geshems that tried so many times to bring him down.

Many accusations were made concerning Pappy. There were those who thought he was too easy, and on one occasion, he was told he was incompetent, but that did not stop him. By prayer and self-control, he was able to overcome everything the adversary sent his way.

When his enemies said his hands were weak, he prayed as Nehemiah prayed, "Now therefore O God, strengthen my hands." I know for a fact that the Lord did strengthen his hands and allow those to come into his life who held on for him and prayed for him.

Being the visionary that he was, Pappy could be compared to the prophet Joel. Joel prophesied that in the last day, God would pour out His spirit upon all flesh and Pappy believed and taught that before the Lord would return, the church, which is us, would see a mighty outpouring of the Spirit of the Lord upon the church.

He even prophesied that many ministries would be birthed, and today as we watch the many television ministers who have come forth; we see one of the many prophesies that have come to pass.

Yes, Pappy saw into the future as the prophet Isaiah did, and he told the church to awake and put on our strength along with our beautiful garments. He believed the words of Isaiah that no weapon that was formed against him would prosper.

As I saw the great faith he had, I could see the "Father Abraham" part of him. It seemed as if he was on a great journey. He was always looking for that land that the Lord had shown him. He had to rescue those who were with him many times. It seemed like he was always going behind the scenes, working to free someone out of their spiritual Sodom and Gomorrah.

Pappy's Eternal Impact

Many times, his enemies were scratching their heads; they didn't know how to take him. Often he and I would discuss what had been said and done by those who didn't see eye to eye with him, and he would say, "Son, don't let them draw your fire; don't let them know where your fire is coming from." I knew it had to be God guiding him, for I was of the opinion I would let them see where the fire was coming from and give them a good dose of fire to remember me by.

Allow me to say that now as I have grown in my Christian walk, I find those instructions to be of great value. You can't always fire back because with every action there is a reaction. But he would always say, "Son, one day you'll understand where I'm coming from." As I think about it, I was quite young in the ministry at that time, but as time went on, I grasped some of his philosophy, and it does work. After over 25 years in the ministry, I am beginning to see where he was coming from.

Once I heard someone say, "Bishop's compassion for people will kill him." I won't say his compassion and love for people killed him, but I will say it put a great deal of pressure on him as he aged. He was always careful not to hurt anyone; he actually put his feelings on hold and looked out for everybody except himself.

Pappy - As Human as They Come

Do not think I am trying to make a "god" out of Pappy, for Pappy was a human being who, like all of us, had the usual human traits and shortcomings that go along with the pressures and issues of life. Job made mistakes, as we all do. I am sure Pappy made his share of mistakes. I know he had his issues as all of us have. We all have made them, and if the truth was told, there are those who are still making mistakes.

In his lifetime, Pappy heard things that were said, but he never let it keep him down. On many occasions in his last days, I saw him weep bitterly because he felt he was a failure, but I did what he taught me to do, that which he had instilled in me. I would offer encouragement, prayer, and understanding. I watched him so many times as he would reach down within and pull from his reservoir of resilience, put on that million-dollar smile, and continue on. He always taught and believed that a child of God had something within them to cause them to always bounce back. He was an awesome example of how to be human yet spiritual. Pappy. He was indeed a great man of God.

PRECIOUS MEMORIES

I trust you have gained some insight and comfort as you have read my heartfelt encounters and insight about the late, great Bishop Quander Lear Wilson, Sr. He was my father, my mentor, my friend, as well as my pastor – the man who I think was a man before his time.

The pictures and accolades on the following pages are presented here as a further tribute to Bishop Wilson. Many of the memories are pictures and documents that have been stored through the years and show the wear and tear thereof. However, they were precious to Bishop Wilson and me, and hopefully you will understand that the desire to share them with you overshadowed their present-day condition. Know that he loved you dearly and perhaps some of the memories will cause you to smile.

Hear the EVANGELISTIC DUO from Ohio

Rev. Q.L. Wilson   Rev. W.W.Smith
The Young, Dynamic Gospel Preachers, Singers and
Musicians, in a Great

SOUL SAVING CAMPAIGN

At ALLEYNE A.M.E.Z. Church
56th & Vine Streets, Philadelphia, Pa.

Beginning Sunday, June 15, 1941
And ending with Laying of the Corner Stone

Preaching and Good Spiritual Singing Every Night!

Come and Join us in Prayer and Consecration for
a Mighty Revival and Spiritual Uplift.

EVERYBODY WELCOME

Hear the Rehoboth Gospel Chorus, of Elmwood,
United Gospel Singers' Assn., and a Special Chorus.

REV. R. M. H. FLETCHER, Pastor.

The Dynamic Duo

Dr. M. L. King and Bishop Q. L. Wilson, Sr.
(Interviewed on WAMO Radio in Pittsburgh, PA)

Quander Lear Wilson, Jr.
(Son)

Bishop and Larry
Father and Son

Quander Jr. and wife Gwen

Quander Lear Wilson III
Grandson

Edward and Rose Marie Shouse
(Son and daughter-in-law)

Granddaughters Loretta and Anissa
Grandson EJ

Nevaeh A. Shouse
Great-granddaughter

Quander L. Shouse
Great-grandson

Mr. and Mrs. Quander L. Wilson, III
and
Bishop Wilson's great-grandsons

Mr. and Mrs. Mark Counts and family
Bishop Wilson's grandson and great-grandchildren

Bishop and Mother Wilson
Banquet time

Son, Father, Grandson

We Are Family
Quander III, Loretta, Gwen, Eddie, Sr., Mark

Two who served as Bishop's caregiver, driver, and administrator
Bishop Stephen and Lady Loretta

Bishop C.M. Grant and Bishop Wilson
Two pioneers of Greater Emmanuel

Bishop Wilson and one of his drivers, Elder Frank Watkins

Celebration Time

Pappy and Frank "chilling"

Bishop and Mother Isabella Rowe

Bishop preaching to the saints

Bishop believed in the "laying on of hands" for deliverance and healing

A preacher of the gospel

Bishop back in the day in Portsmouth, Ohio

Telling it like it is!

Bishop Stacy Roberts - Bishop's nephew
and Bishop Edward Shouse

The following pages contain copies of a few of Bishop Wilson's many achievements, events, and community recognitions, both local and national.

CREDENTIALS

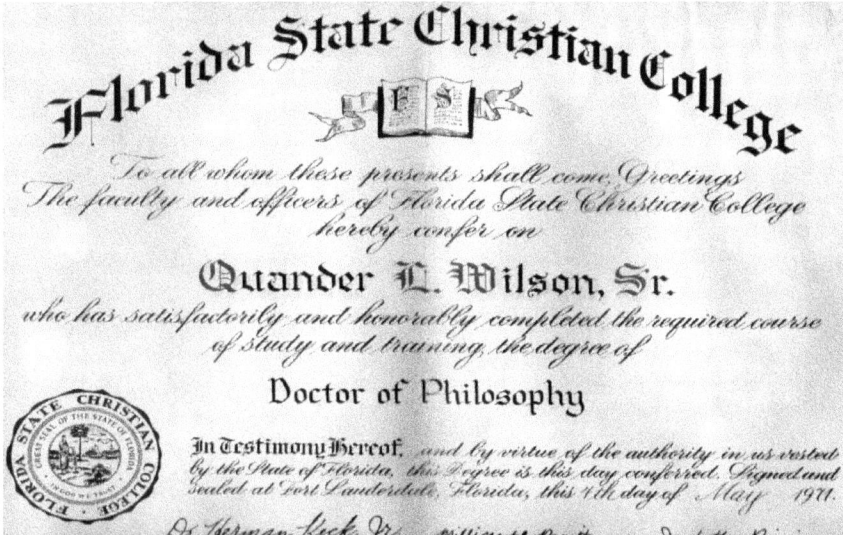

Bishop Wilson's Doctor of Philosophy Degree

Greater Emmanuel International Fellowship, Inc.

Book No. 1   Page No. 1

Certificate of Fellowship License

Endeavoring to keep the unity of the spirit in the bond of peace.
Ephesians 4:3

This certifies that **BISHOP QUANDER L. WILSON, SR.** of 3240 Haskell Drive, Columbus, OH 43219 is an Ordained Bishop in good standing with the above named affiliation. This license remains the property of the organization and subject to recall if status changes.

Interval Period: Yearly Renewal   Date Issued: 07/01/02

Authorizing Signature   Title

A FEW MOMENTOS

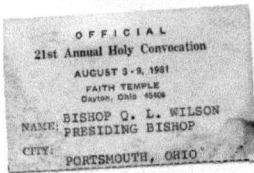

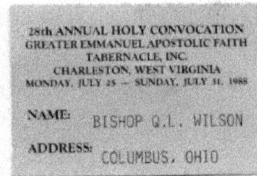

1991 NATIONAL PASTORS CONFERENCE
Bishop
Quander
Wilson
Columbus,
Ohio
Greater Life Evangelistic Center
Plenary Speaker
The Church of the 1990s: What God is Saying

OFFICIAL
21st Annual Holy Convocation
AUGUST 3 - 9, 1981
FAITH TEMPLE
Dayton, Ohio 45406
NAME: BISHOP Q. L. WILSON
PRESIDING BISHOP
CITY: PORTSMOUTH, OHIO

28th ANNUAL HOLY CONVOCATION
GREATER EMMANUEL APOSTOLIC FAITH
TABERNACLE, INC.
CHARLESTON, WEST VIRGINIA
MONDAY, JULY 25 — SUNDAY, JULY 31, 1988
NAME: BISHOP Q.L. WILSON
ADDRESS: COLUMBUS, OHIO

Brings back memories, huh?

Harvesters' Fellowship '84
BISHOP QUANDER WILSON
FELLOWSHIP MINISTER

14th
ANNUAL
Y. P. F. E.
CONVENTION
G.E.A.F.T., Inc.
JUNE 16 - 18, 1978
"YOUTH DEDICATING
THEIR LIVES TO GOD"
R. McDONALD WORTHAM
D.D., President

GREATER
EMANUEL
APOSTOLIC
CHURCH
10TH
WOMEN'S
CONVENTION
1978

Greater Emmanuel International Fellowship of Churches and Ministries Inc.,

Certificate of Appreciation

to

Dr. Quander L. Wilson, Sr., Chief Apostle

It is with extreme gratification the National Women's Department of the Greater Emmanuel International Fellowship of Churches and Ministries present to you this publication, in admiration of the tremendous contribution you have made in leadership. Reverently, we say THANK YOU for your perpetual dedication in the administration of God's word to us. We are indebted for your devout, self-sacrificing time you've exhausted ministering, (praying, fasting, sharing, and caring), just for us. The book of better things convey the sentiments of our heart, "For God is not unrighteous to forget your work and labour of love, which ye have shewed toward His name, in that ye have ministered to the Saints, and do minister." We beseech that as you peruse through the pages of this booklet, you will find fortitude and encouragement today and in the future.

Presented this Eighteenth day of May, Ninteen Hundred and Ninety One

The National Women's Department

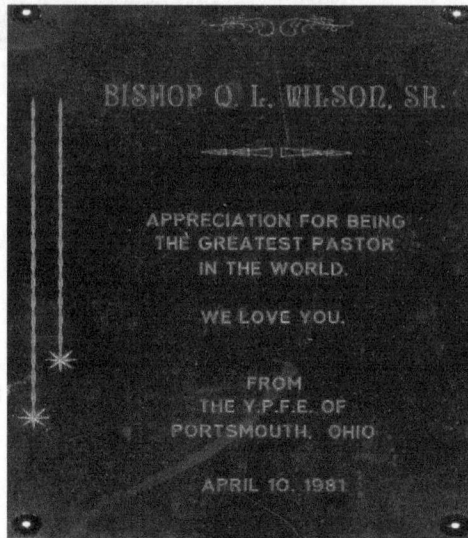

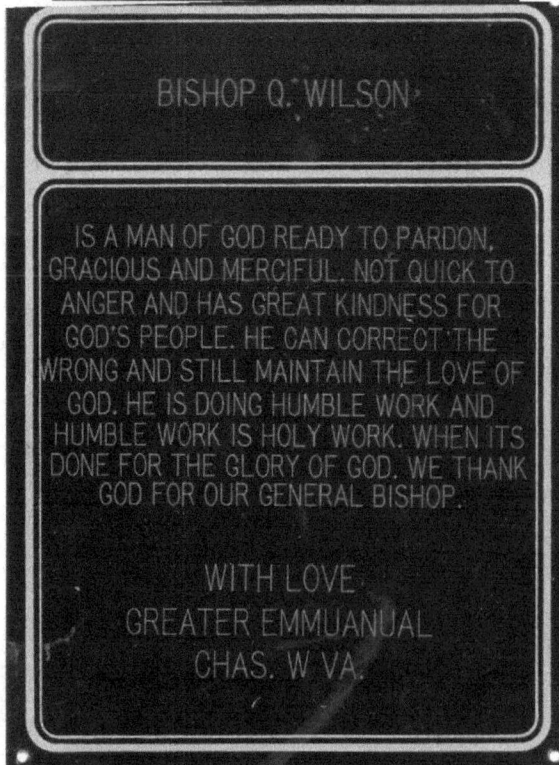

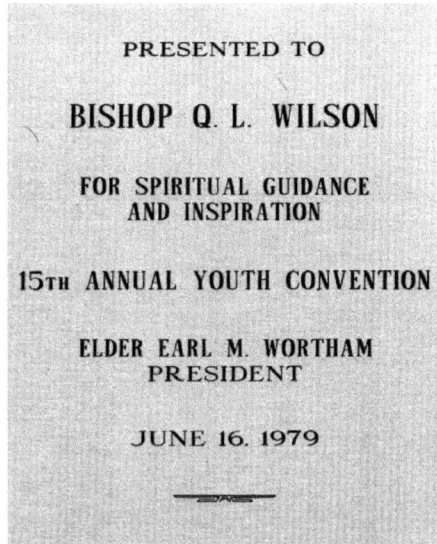

PRESENTED TO

BISHOP Q. L. WILSON

FOR SPIRITUAL GUIDANCE
AND INSPIRATION

15TH ANNUAL YOUTH CONVENTION

ELDER EARL M. WORTHAM
PRESIDENT

JUNE 16, 1979

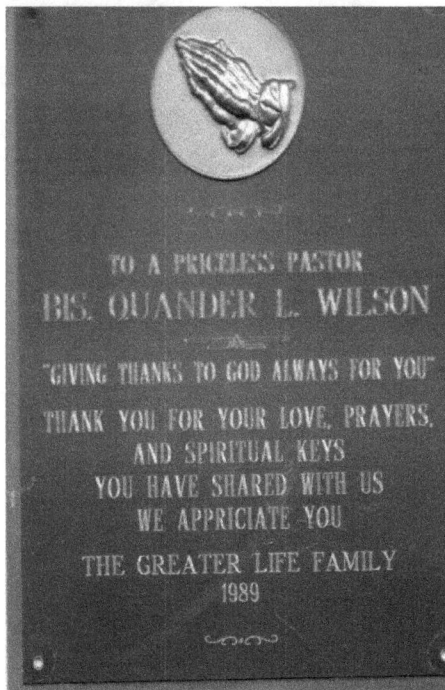

TO A PRICELESS PASTOR
BIS. QUANDER L. WILSON

"GIVING THANKS TO GOD ALWAYS FOR YOU"

THANK YOU FOR YOUR LOVE, PRAYERS,
AND SPIRITUAL KEYS
YOU HAVE SHARED WITH US
WE APPRICIATE YOU

THE GREATER LIFE FAMILY
1989

AWARDED TO

BISHOP QUANDER L. WILSON

IN APPRECIATION AND LOVE

FROM
THE DEACON BOARD
OF
GREATER EMMANUEL CHURCH
PORTSMOUTH, OHIO
8/18/74

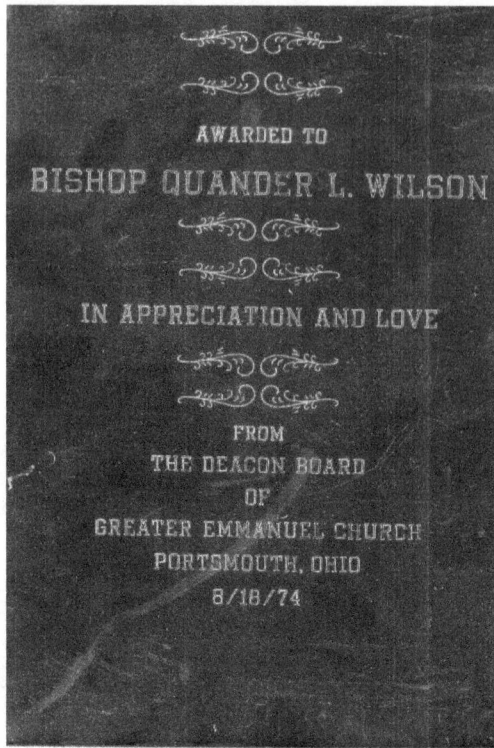

City of Columbus
Office of the Mayor
Certificate
of

Honor & Recognition

Presented To

BISHOP Q.L. AND MARY WILSON

For your outstanding service to the citizens of

Columbus and for your 3rd Pastor's Appreciation.

Dana G. Rinehart, Mayor

March 19, 1990

Date

Columbus City Council
CERTIFICATE
of
HONOR AND RECOGNITION
to

BISHOP O. L. WILSON AND MRS. MARY WILSON

for

THE OCCASION OF THEIR

THIRD PASTOR'S APPRECIATION

Introduced by:

Member of Council   APRIL 1, 1990
Date

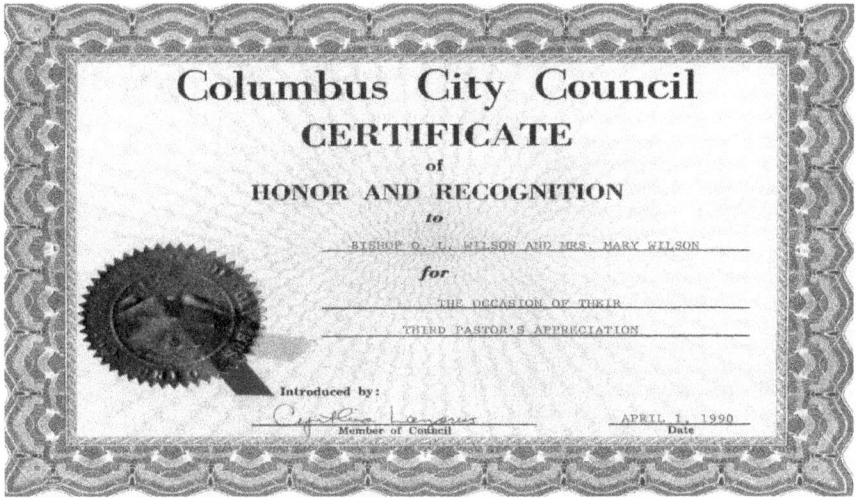

ON CHAMPION AND TORONTO

On Champion and Toronto, there stands an edifice,
called "GREATER LIFE EVANGELISTIC TEMPLE", one of
GOD'S chosen, one of his best. To slay the wicked one,
yet, uphold the forlorned. Yes, on Champion and Toronto
stands one of God's select.

On Champion and Toronto, The Holy Ghost abides,
there HE does GOD'S bidding, bringing dead men
to life.

On Champion and Toronto, GOD stamps his very own,
with his grace and his mercy and his power to go
on. Filled with his Holy Spirit to set the
captive free, on Champion and Toronto, GOD is
there for you and me.

On Champion and Toronto, come visit when you can!
You'll find God still abiding, waiting for your
outstretched hands...On Champion and Toronto.

                              6JUN94
                              C.I. CORNELIOUS

123

COLUMBUS CITY COUNCIL

JERRY HAMMOND, *PRESIDENT*
CYNTHIA LAZARUS, *PRESIDENT PRO TEM*

BEN ESPY
THOMAS L. KAPLIN
JOHN P. KENNEDY
M.D. PORTMAN
ARLENE SHOEMAKER

City Hall
90 West Broad Street
Columbus, Ohio 43215-4184
614/645-7380   FAX 614/645-6164

CITY CLERK
Timothy McSweeney

LEGISLATIVE RESEARCH OFFICE
Charles A. Mentel, Manager

April 1, 1990

Bishop Q. L. Wilson
Greater Life Evangelistic Temple
487 N. Champion Avenue
Columbus, Ohio 43203

Dear Bishop Wilson:

I regret that I will be unable to join you and your beloved wife Mary on this occasion of your Third Pastor's Appreciation Observance.

I do, however, want to offer both of you my warmest congratulations. Please also accept my prayers and best wishes as you continue to guide the spiritual needs of your congregation. May God richly bless you both.

Sincerely,

CYNTHIA LAZARUS
Member of Council

CL:bmt

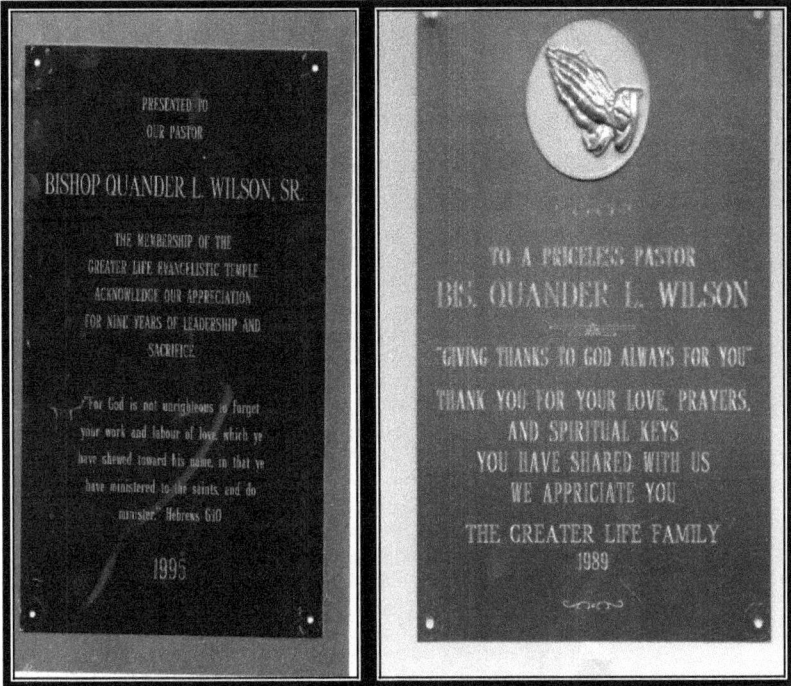

ACCOLADES OF LOVE

Tribute to Dad

I met Bishop Wilson over 40 years ago. I can remember the first time I saw him, we were watching what we now call videos. At that time they were called "home movies", the old fashion reel type movies.

While watching him in a film at the Diocese Meeting in Detroit, Michigan, I inquired as to whom this man was. I was told he was the District Elder of the Original Glorious Church. I never dreamed that he would become my father. Now that I think about it, I did say to myself, I wish he was my dad. In later years, the Lord sent him to a little country church in Burlington, Ohio to run a revival, it was there that I received the Holy Ghost through his ministry and our relationship began.

As time moved on, I became his adopted son, along with his biological son Larry. He and his wife Mother Mary Wilson took me in their family, and from then until now; I learned what a family was all about, the responsibility of manhood and the responsibility of being a husband and father. It has been an experience, but a pleasant one, although I had to learn how to be a son and how to accept life through the teachings and example he laid down for me.

I could write a book just on the times we have shared, from learning how to drive a bus to towing him on a solid sheet of ice and forgetting he was behind me. I still can remember how big his eyes became as I was towing him on this icy road.

For us not to have biological blood, I think we are similar. Sometimes that poses a problem. I would like to do things another way, but because I have been around him so long, I find myself walking in his footsteps to a degree. That is when I find that his foot prints are so large that one would have to live 100 years to begin to fill them.

I am grateful to the Lord for the spirit of this man that can only come from God, this spirit was, this spirit is, and will always be "the wind beneath my wings." I am determined to be the best son of all sons to him, using all that he has taught me.

As I listen to those he has influenced and mentored along the way, their manner of delivery, the things they say, their ideas - I hear and see the spirit of my father, Bishop Wilson, speaking and moving. He continues to live on.

I watched him push others, they have soared and continue to soar, because the spirit of my Dad remains as the wind that is never seen but is so important.

When I see others moving forward, I say to myself, that's "Pappy" they may never own up to it, but when they do whatever they do and it is a positive move, I see "Pappy".

There is a special light in my home today
It's all because of you my wonderful dad;
There's a special place in my heart today,
For the best dad a man could ever have.
I will always have a tribute of love,
in my heart every night, every day, even this day
For the grand things you have done for me and my family;
May the God of all peace reward you for
all the good works you have accomplished
while on this earth My Wonderful Dad

This man is the Patriarch of the Shouse family,
we love him, and we respect him.
We will always remember him as such.

Certificate of Special Congressional Recognition

Presented to

Dr. Quander L. Wilson Sr.

in recognition of outstanding and invaluable service to the community.

7/26/02
DATE

MEMBER OF CONGRESS

COLUMBUS CITY COUNCIL

CERTIFICATE
OF
HONOR AND RECOGNITION

IN CELEBRATION OF THE LIFE & MINISTRY OF

DR. QUANDER LEAR WILSON, SR

WHEREAS, Dr. Quander Lear Wilson, Sr., answered the "call" to the Christian ministry in the year of 1937; and

WHEREAS, on January 27, 1980, Dr. Wilson answered a more urgent call of GOD's people to pastor Greater Life Evangelistic Temple, and, through his love, teaching & devotion to GOD led them to their first church home on April 27, 1986; and

WHEREAS, Dr. Wilson through his dedication to nurture and guide the saints to greater spiritual knowledge & love of GOD has inspired constant and unfolding growth as founder of Chief Apostle of the Greater Emmanuel International, Inc.; and

WHEREAS, Dr. Wilson is internationally recognized as a teacher, Preacher & Visionary; has been published and continues to spiritually inspire all those whose lives he touches.

THEREFORE BE IT FURTHER RESOLVED, that we Praise Dr. Quander L. Wilson, Sr., on his 81st birthday and give thanks that the LORD has blessed us with his love and guidance the past 62 years.

INTRODUCED BY:

MICHAEL B. COLEMAN, PRESIDENT

JULY 1, 1999

THE WORTH OF A MAN

The worth of a man is not measured by the materialistic things that he gains,
but is measured by what he gives.

The worth of a man is not measured by receiving all the accolades and applause,
but by always giving them.

The worth of a man is not measured by the vanity of one's flesh,
but it is measured by a true sense of spirituality in communion with God.

This is the worth of a man...

Always true to himself, so he can be true to others

Always giving never taking

Always reaching and pulling others

This is the worth of a man

This is your worth

We Love You!

Greater Emmanuel International Fellowship, Inc.

BOB TAFT
GOVERNOR
STATE OF OHIO

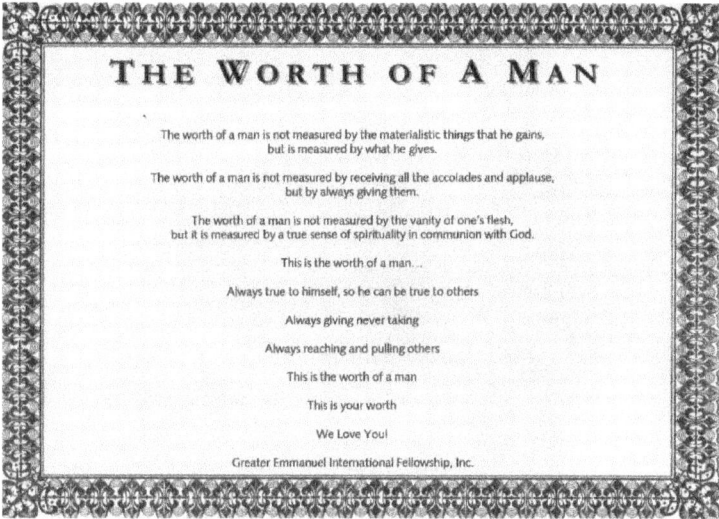

IN RECOGNITION OF
DR. QUANDER L. WILSON, SR.

I am pleased to extend my warmest greetings and congratulations to Dr. Quander L. Wilson, Sr. as you are honored for your more than sixty-five years of service to the Christian Ministry.

Ohio churches have traditionally been the bedrock of our society. I am humbled by the churches' daily work that has truly been a testament to members' faith in God and love for humanity. Always conscious of the needs of the larger community, local church fellowships devote considerable time working toward the betterment of their neighborhood. In your years of service to the Greater Life Evangelistic Temple congregation, your Church and its members have exhibited strength, dedication, and a true devotion to their faith.

On behalf of all Ohioans, best wishes on this special day, and may the joy and goodwill that surround you today continue throughout the years to come!

Sincerely,

Bob Taft

Bob Taft
Governor

77 SOUTH HIGH STREET · 30TH FLOOR · COLUMBUS, OHIO 43215-6117 · 614.466.3555 · FAX: 614.466.9354

CARLTON D. PEARSON

July 25, 2002

Bishop Quander Wilson
487 N. Champion Ave.
Columbus, OH 43203

Dear Bishop Wilson:

Grace and peace from God the Father and Christ Jesus our Savior!

Congratulations good and faithful servant! Gina and I wanted to let you know that we are rejoicing with you as you celebrate *"66 years of Christian Ministry." Wow!* What an accomplishment. To God be the glory for the great things He has done in you and through you for 66 years.

Although Gina and I are unable to attend the banquet that is planned in your honor, we salute you on this momentous occasion. We honor you for your unselfish ministry and mark of excellence that has touched so many lives including my own. You are a General in the Body of Christ.

Gina and I join with others in expressing our love and support. You deserve all of the accolades coming to you. Our prayers are with you for many more years of *anointed* and *excellent* ministry.

You have proven that you have what it takes to finish your course with joy! Champions are not those who never fail, they are those who never quit. Failing isn't the worst thing that could happen to you—quitting is. You are on your way to a *wealthy place in God!*

May our Lord Jesus Christ Himself and God our Father encourage your heart and strengthen you in every good deed and word. The Lord is with you and so are we!

Your Best is Yet to Come,

Bishop Carlton D. Pearson, DD

CDP/dmw

Enclosure

P.O. BOX 700007 ■ TULSA, OKLAHOMA 74170 ■ (918) 250-0483 ■ FAX (918) 2

STATE OF WEST VIRGINIA
OFFICE OF THE GOVERNOR
CHARLESTON 25305

BOB WISE
GOVERNOR

CONGRATULATIONS FROM THE GOVERNOR

to

Dr. Quander L. Wilson, Sr.

As Governor of the state of West Virginia, it is my pleasure to extend my sincere congratulations and best wishes to you for your 65 years of ministering and pastoral services to the people of the West Virginia and Ohio.

Through your dedicated teachings and ministering, you have touched the lives of many people. As a respected evangelist, published author and founder of the Greater Emmanuel International Church and Ministry, you have provided faithful service and dedicated yourself to the spiritual health and well-being of your many parishioners. The personal satisfaction of knowing you have enriched the lives of countless people cannot be measured.

Again, thank you for your tremendous contributions. My best wishes to you on this special occasion.

Very truly yours,

Bob Wise
Governor

JOHN D. ROCKEFELLER IV
WEST VIRGINIA

United States Senate

WASHINGTON, DC 20510–4802

July 26, 2002

Dear Dr. Wilson,

I would like to commend you today for your 65 years of service to the ministry. Your unwavering dedication has allowed you to touch the lives of many. Therefore, I know I am not alone in celebrating this very special anniversary.

From the first sermon you delivered in 1937 to the Doctorate in Theology you received in 1971, you have lived a life of service rich in accomplishment. In an historic century full of change, you have helped to unite people of all backgrounds; this has allowed them to better themselves and their communities. For this and for many other reasons, you should be enormously proud of your achievements.

I am delighted to have shared part of this occasion with you, Dr. Wilson. Best wishes and every good thing to you in the future.

Sincerely,

John D. Rockefeller IV

http://rockefeller.senate.gov

MAXINE WATERS
MEMBER OF CONGRESS
35TH DISTRICT, CALIFORNIA

July 26, 2002

Dr. Quander L. Wilson, Sr.
Greater Life Evangelistic Temple
Columbus, Ohio

Dear Dr. Wilson,

Congratulations on celebrating 65 years in the ministry. I hope your day is exciting as you continue to use your leadership to promote the Lord's work.

Your message has helped thousands find salvation and deliverance. You have been hailed as a visionary, a Chief Apostle, a pioneer of Christian ministry and a communicator of the gospel through the published word.

I am delighted at age 85, you continue to evangelize across the nation and still serve as Senior Pastor of the Greater Life Evangelistic Temple.

Please accept my best wishes for continued success.

Sincerely,

Maxine Waters

MAXINE WATERS
MEMBER of CONGRESS

UNITED STATES SENATE
WASHINGTON, D. C.

ORRIN G. HATCH
UTAH

July 26, 2002

Dear Dr. Wilson:

I understand that you are being honored this year after sixty-five years in the ministry. It is my pleasure to congratulate you on this great achievement. I join your family and friends in honoring you for your distinguished service in preaching the gospel.

This is truly something to celebrate, not only for you and your family, but for all those who know you. Your love of life is an example to us all. Congratulations on this joyous and memorable occasion and best wishes for the years to come.

Sincerely,

Orrin G. Hatch
United States Senator

Dr. Quander L. Wilson Sr.
1740 North 285 West
Layton, UT 84041

GEORGE V. VOINOVICH
OHIO

317 HART SENATE OFFICE BUILDING
(202) 224-3353
TDD: (202) 224-6997
for_voinovich@voinovich.senate.gov
http://voinovich.senate.gov

United States Senate

WASHINGTON, DC 20510-3504

GOVERNMENTAL AFFAIRS
RANKING MEMBER, SUBCOMMITTEE O
OVERSIGHT OF GOVERNMENT MANAGEME
RESTRUCTURING AND THE
DISTRICT OF COLUMBIA

ENVIRONMENT AND
PUBLIC WORKS
RANKING MEMBER,
SUBCOMMITTEE ON CLEAN AIR, WETLAT
AND CLIMATE CHANGE

ETHICS

IN RECOGNITION OF
REV. DR. QUANDER L. WILSON, SR.
FOR HIS MANY YEARS IN THE MINISTRY
JULY 26, 2002

I am pleased to extend my warmest greetings to Rev. Dr. Quander L. Wilson, Sr. who has dedicated his life to ministry and community service.

In your years of working in the ministry, you have been an inspiration to many. You touched the lives of many by making yourself available to those who were hurting and to those who had no without hope or direction. Your gift for bridging the gap between denominational and racial lines caused reconciliation in the lives of thousands across our country. Your congregation should feel exceptionally fortunate to be blessed by your service.

I join with your wife, Mary Helen, and your entire family in recognizing your many years in the ministry. May God continue to bless you.

Sincerely,

George V. Voinovich
United States Senator

STATE OFFICES:
36 EAST SEVENTH STREET
ROOM 2615
CINCINNATI, OHIO 45202
(513) 684-3265

1240 EAST NINTH STREET
ROOM 2955
CLEVELAND, OHIO 44199
(216) 522-7095

37 WEST BROAD STREET
ROOM 320 (CASEWORK)
COLUMBUS, OHIO 43215
(614) 469-6774

37 WEST BROAD STREET
ROOM 310
COLUMBUS, OHIO 43215
(614) 469-6697

420 MADISON
ROOM 1210
TOLEDO, OHIO
(419) 259-34

PRINTED ON RECYCLED PAPER

135

THE WHITE HOUSE

WASHINGTON

July 24, 2002

The Reverend Quander L. Wilson, D.D.
Greater Life Evangelistic Temple
Columbus, Ohio

Dear Dr. Wilson:

Congratulations on celebrating your 65th anniversary in the ministry.
This milestone provides a wonderful opportunity for your family, friends,
and parishioners to recognize you for your many accomplishments.

A strong spiritual foundation is central to the lives of Americans. By
sharing God's teachings with your congregation, you have enriched
the lives of countless individuals and served as an inspiration to the
community. Our Nation is a better place because of your dedication
to sharing your wisdom, guidance, and faith with others.

Laura joins me in sending best wishes on this special occasion.

Sincerely,

George W. Bush

** TOTAL PAGE

136

And he shall be like a tree planted by the rivers of water, that bringeth forth his fruit in his season; his leaf also shall not wither; and whatsoever he doeth shall prosper.
Psalms 1:3

Bishop Quander L. Wilson

I count it a pleasure to speak of the treasure, we have at Greater Life!
He's the water that nourishes, through the Word that encourages each one of us to
continue to meet challenges in the face of tribulation and strife.
He's admired by those he's inspired, to trod this journey for God.
He's anointed and appointed, a man in demand.
In faraway places, he's known for his stand.
Sanctioned with the authority of scriptural text.
He's devil stompin' with a spiritual flex.
With the muscle of faith and the power of the Word,
He's spreading the good news like you've never heard!
Everybody sees, but only a few know.
Everybody talks the journey, but few want to go --
to the heights and depths that God can take them to.
But this man has been there and back, time and again,
praying and binding, and delivering God's plan.
Through many tears and fifty years of earnest supplication,
with dedication uprooting sin with a spiritual indignation.
Undefeated, Quander L. Wilson has held fast and true.
He's blessed with the Wisdom of Solomon, the Courage of David,
the Conviction of Daniel and the Faith of Abraham.
His unique style and winning smile spans the ages, young and old.
So I count it a pleasure, to speak of this treasure,
Chief Apostle Quander L. Wilson, he's gold!
"Behind every man there's a good woman", at least that's what they say,
But I beg to differ, because proudly beside him there is Mama Mae.
His hand to hold, his treasure, his gold, without her mention my saying is incomplete.
She's there for his ups, she's there for his downs, making his life a little more sweet.
Bishop, from this day forward, no poems, no flowers, no empty words --
In the most important ways you'll know,
With kingdom living and kingdom principles, our actions and deeds will show,
That we love you much and need you more.
A better leader we couldn't have had,
We give you this homage because we know,
"It's a poor frog that won't croak on his own pad!"

Written by: M. Darlene Hammond
Dollhouse Inspirations

Precious Memories

To: My Pappy - Dr. Q. L. Wilson

When god said I want you to help me - Some years ago - I can amagine you saying - yes lord yes to your will and to your way - so you started out on this narrow rugged road - sometimes up and sometime down - almost level to the ground - you've been lied on - cheated - talked about - mistreated - I can also amagine you saying - But as long as I've got King Jesus I don't need nobody else - we fall down - but we get up - and you would say - so I'm climbing up the rough side of the mountian - I'm doing my best to make it in - So I need you to walk with me lord - walk with me - Hold my hand lord - please hold my hand - while I'm on this tedious Journey - I need you Jesus to walk with me so on ward Christian soldier - you climb because you know that every round goes Higher and Higher - and 99 1/2 won't do - gatta make 100 - thinking all the way - Jesus I'll never forget how you set me free - Jesus I'll never forget how you brought me out - Jesus I'll never forget no never - I can amagine trouble was in your way - you had to cry sometimes - you laid awake as at night I can hear you say - But that's Alright - I know Jesus will fix it after while - and I'll understand it better by and by - But for now - I'll keep climbing one more round higher till I reach the top - because I've got a feeling - everythings gonna be alright - Be alright - Be alright - you see I had no earthy Dad to teach me how to climb - I thank god you saw me 42 years ago - struggling far behind you reachout - and put your hand in minde - thanks to you I'm Still here - I'm get Holding on .

Thank you
From your Daughter
Sister Babare Davis

(aunt Barb)
March 31. 2002

ON CHAMPION AND TORONTO

On Champion and Toronto, there stands an edifice,
called "GREATER LIFE EVANGELISTIC TEMPLE", one of
GOD'S chosen, one of his best. To slay the wicked one,
yet, uphold the forlorned. Yes, on Champion and Toronto,
stands one of God's select.

On Champion and Toronto, The Holy Ghost abides,
there HE does GOD'S bidding, bringing dead men
to life.

On Champion and Toronto, GOD stamps his very own,
with his grace and his mercy and his power to go
on. Filled with his Holy Spirit to set the
captive free, on Champion and Toronto, GOD is
there for you and me.

On Champion and Toronto, come visit when you can!
You'll find God still abiding, waiting for your
outstretched hands...On Champion and Toronto.

6JUN94
C.I. CORNELIOUS

ACQUISITION. The Portsmouth Inner City Development Corp. has acquired its first property under the Findlay St. Redevelopment Program at 1302 Kinney St. from Dorothy Calloway. Taking part in the transaction were (left to right) Harvey Richardson, acquisition manager; Walter Lytten, attorney; Bishop Q. L. Wilson, treasurer; Dorothy Calloway; Keith Scott, housing resources manager, and E. P. Matthews, executive director.

139

PROMISE YOURSELF

Promise yourself to be so strong that nothing can disturb your peace of mind. To talk health, happiness and prosperity to every person you meet. To make all your friends feel that there is something in them. To look at the sunny side of everything and make your optimism come true. To think only of the best, to work only for the best, and expect only the best. To be just as enthusiastic about the success of others as you are about your own. To forget the mistakes of the past and press on to greater achievements of the future. To wear a cheerful countenance at all times and give every living creature you meet a smile. To give so much time to the improvement of yourself that you have no time to criticize others. To be too large for worry, too noble for anger, too strong for fear and too happy to permit the presence of trouble.

Christian D. Larson

Bishop T.D. Jakes

MARCH 2002

BISHOP QUANDER L. WILSON
GREATER LIFE EVANGELISTIC TEMPLE
487 NORTH CHAMPION AVENUE
COLUMBUS, OH 43203

DEAR BISHOP WILSON:

IT IS WITH GREAT JOY THAT WE SEND OUR LOVE, PRAYERS AND
CONGRATULATIONS TO YOU FOR THE MANY YEARS OF UNSELFISH SACRIFICE
THAT YOU HAVE GIVEN IN MINISTRY.

THE BIBLE DECLARES IN *HEB 6:10, "FOR GOD IS NOT UNRIGHTEOUS TO FORGET
YOUR WORK AND LABOUR OF LOVE, WHICH YE HAVE SHEWED TOWARD HIS
NAME, IN THAT YE HAVE MINISTERED TO THE SAINTS, AND DO MINISTER."*
(KJV) WHAT AN AWESOME RESULT OF THE WORK YOU ARE RENDERING IN THE
KINGDOM, SHOWN BY THOSE WHO LOVE AND CARE ENOUGH TO HONOR YOU.
YOU ARE A GREAT ASSET AMONG THE BODY OF BELIEVERS THAT WORK IN
THE VINEYARD.

ON BEHALF OF MY WIFE, SERITA AND I, ALONG WITH OUR STAFF AND CHURCH
FAMILY, WE WOULD LIKE TO EXTEND THE CHOICEST OF BLESSINGS UPON YOU
AND YOUR ENTIRE FAMILY.

IN HIS SERVICE,

BISHOP T.D. JAKES, SR.
SENIOR PASTOR
THE POTTER'S HOUSE OF DALLAS, INC.

The Potter's House
6777 West Kiest Boulevard • Dallas, Texas 75236 • 214-331-0954

OFFICE OF THE MAYOR
COLUMBUS

CERTIFICATE
of
RECOGNITION

PRESENTED TO:

Pastor Quander Wilson

in Honor of

**11 years as Pastor of
Greater Life Evangelistic Temple**

On behalf of the citizens of the City of Columbus, we commend you and express our appreciation for your contributions to the welfare of our community. Under your leadership, the Greater Life Evangelistic Temple has grown in its ability to minister to the needs of our people. We wish you continued success in every endeavor.

November 13, 1994

Gregory S. Lashutka
Mayor

BISHOP QUANDER L. WILSON

.....He is a chosen vessel unto me, to bear my name..., Acts 9:15

Job had patience, Solomon had gold,
Isaiah had visions in the Bible days of old.
Jeremiah was a weeping prophet, Ezekiel's God was the wheel,
With a sling shot and a rock the giant David did kill.
Now, John was the beloved disciple and Joshua's battle God did win,
and Daniel was delivered from the lion's den.
Abraham was the Father of Nations, Peter the fisher of men,
And Dr. Q. L. Wilson is a modern day prophet on whom God can depend.
I stand today to speak of one of the greatest minds on the theological horizon,
His principles have facilitated changes that are distinctively revolutionizing.
His persona is understated,
And it's no misconception that his perception is updated.
If I could paint a picture with words so that you can hear what we see,
I'd say he's humble, full of compassion, amiable and a man of integrity.
He's our gift of love, a rock of strength, a spirit led revelator, too,
Anointed for the mission that God has destined Him to do.
He's a religious pioneer whose wisdom exceeds his years,
When it comes to the Bible, his word is viable
And as a friend he is quite reliable.
With tremendous patience, he listens and gives a Father's advice,
And chastises those he loves, with principles based on the teachings of Christ.
Though ostracized and criticized, Bishop Wilson continues to stand,
But we know that praise builds what criticism kills and we thank God for the man!
He's persistent and consistent, a builder of ministries and men~
His character is awesome, Lord, let me say thank you again.
We pay tribute to this magnificent man who is blessed with divine insight,
Sis. Alice Williams described you, she's says you are dynamite!
Bishop Wilson, my mouth's not saying what our hearts can't deliver,
we're glad God gave you to us!
You're our blessing, you're our treasure, we love you, you're simply splendiferous!

Written by: M. Darlene Carson

The Love of His Life

Mother Mary Helen Wilson

A young Mother Wilson

Mother Wilson on the beach in Hawaii

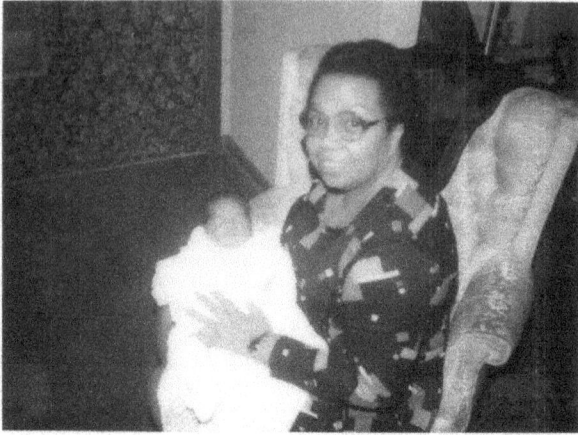

A happy grandmother holding Quander L. Wilson, III

Beautiful couple in their golden years

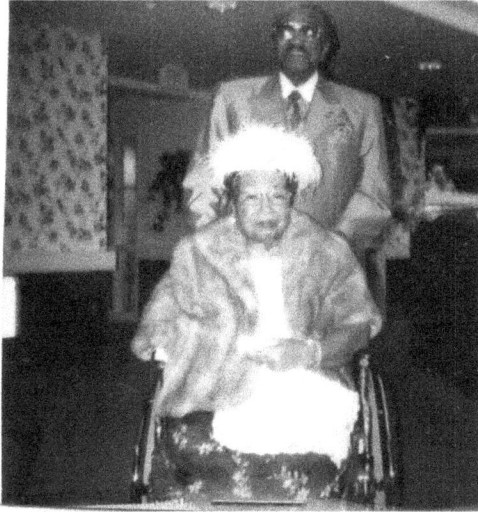

Pappy and Aunt Mae

One of her many awards

Mother Wilson entertaining the saints

CERTIFICATE OF APPRECIATION

Presented To

BISHOP QUANDER & SISTER MARY WILSON

For Outstanding And Dedicated Service As Lovers
of Hospitality, Lovers Of Good Men, Sober Just
Holy Temperate Holding Fast The Fruitful Word

GREATER EMMANUEL INTERNATIONAL FELLOWSHIP
OF CHURCHES AND MINISTRIES, INC.

JULY 27, 1991

"THE LOVE OF HIS LIFE"
BISHOP QUANDER L. WILSON AND
FIRST LADY EVANGELIST MARY H. WILSON

She is clothed with strength and dignity: she can laugh at the days to come.
She speaks with wisdom, and faithful instruction is on her tongue.
Proverbs 31:25-26

THE ROSE M. SHOUSE
HALL OF FAME AWARD

PRESENTED TO

EVANG. MARY H. WILSON

For God Is Not Unrighteous To Forget
Your Work And Labor Of Love...

Hebrews 6:10

Greater Emmanuel International Fellowship
Of Church And Ministries, Inc.

MAY 16, 1992

In Appreciation

This Certificate of Appreciation

is presented to

Mary Wilson
_____

For devoted and faithful service rendered

to __Greater Emmanuel A.F.T._____

as _____Woman of Year_____

_____

May abiding satisfaction be your reward and the years ahead be crowned with God's blessing.

Given this ___22___ day of __August__ 19 71

D. L. L. Wilson L

Mother Gertrude Boyd

To Our Pastor's Wife

When we thank God for our pastor
We must give Him thanks for two,
For when your husband came to us
God also sent us you.

A pastor's wife must be many things,
You have many hats to wear;
And we say thanks for all you do
And lift you up in prayer.

You adjust your life to meet the needs
Of your husband's congregation,
And it seems that you can always cope
With most any situation.

Your presence blesses all of us
Who know you from day to day
As our pastor's wife, you are serving God
In a fine and worthy way.

Helen Bush
Verse and Art © London

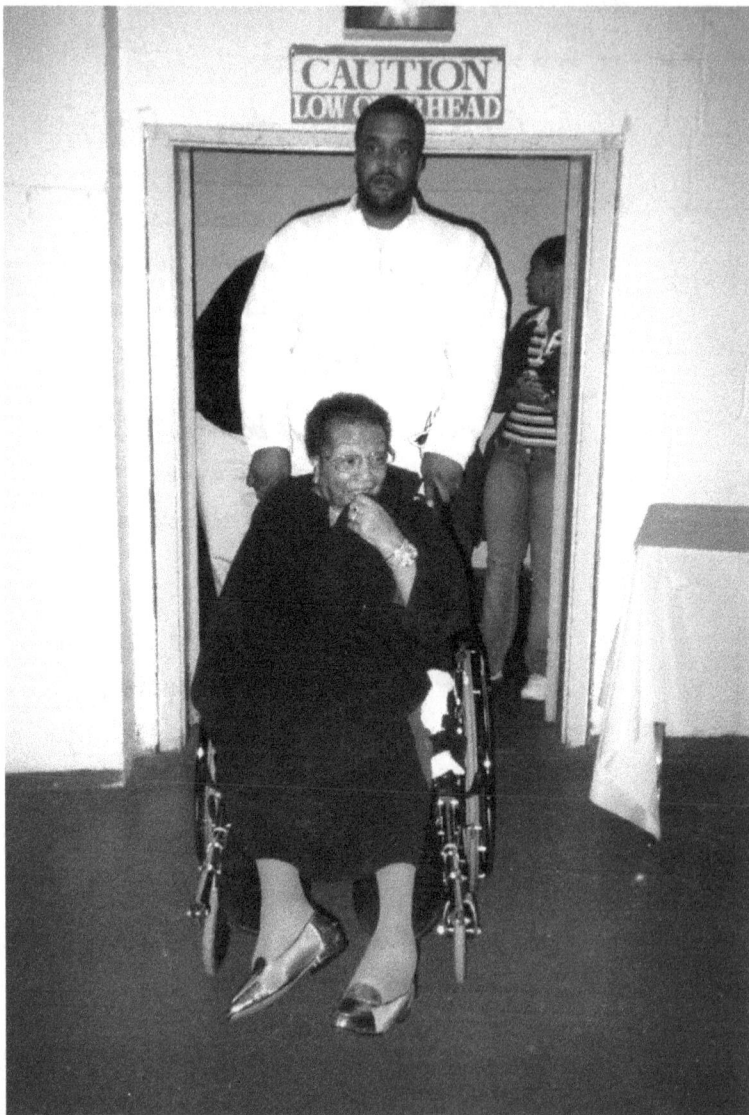

Mother Wilson arriving at one of her birthday parties

CELEBRATING THE LEGACY

Love Always
"PAPPY"

Precious Memories

AUTHOR'S BIOGRAPHICAL SKETCH

Bishop Edward Eugene Shouse, Sr.,
DD, Senior Pastor of the Temple of
Praise, Columbus, Ohio.
Presiding Bishop of the Greater
Emmanuel Fellowship
International, Inc. (GEFI),
Columbus, Ohio.

Bishop Edward E. Shouse, Sr., received Christ at the age of 14. Born in Columbus, Ohio, he was reared for most of his life in the southern part of Ohio, in the community of Burlington, Ohio. He is the son of the late Mother Mary H. Wilson and the late Bishop Quander L. Wilson, Sr. He was educated in the South Point School System, graduating in 1963. He later attended Huntington Business College, majoring in accounting, IBM, and office management.

Bishop Shouse is one of the original young people of the Greater Emmanuel Fellowship, as he has been with the fellowship from its beginning, 59 years ago. He gives the credit first to God, and then to the many precious saints of the Original Glorious Churches in Burlington and

Chillicothe, Ohio, and Huntington, West Virginia, where he was baptized, and received the teachings of the Word of God, and taught the ways of holiness before joining the Greater Emmanuel Fellowship, which laid a godly foundation, which remains solid today.

Bishop Shouse has progressed in rank from church janitor all the way to the office of the Bishop. At the age of 18 he was ordained as a deacon; at age 21 he was ordained as an elder in Greater Emmanuel under the tutelage of his father, Bishop Quander L. Wilson, Sr. In 1989 he was consecrated to the office of Bishop by the College of Bishops of the Greater Emmanuel in the National Holy Convocation in Charleston, West Virginia.

Bishop Shouse has always been active and dedicated to the work of the Lord. He has served in numerous positions within the fellowship from the second national YPFE President, National Music Advisor, Executive Assistant to the Chief Apostle, Chairman of the Executive Board, Jurisdictional Bishop over various states, and now Presiding Bishop and Chief Apostle.

Bishop Shouse served as the pastor of the "Mother Church of Greater Emmanuel," in Portsmouth, Ohio for over 20 years. While there he was recognized by the city of Portsmouth as "The Man with a Vision for Portsmouth." Excerpts from one of his many soul-stirring messages entitled, "Vision and Purpose" was recognized in a national magazine publication. He relinquished his position as pastor of the Portsmouth church in July of 2005.

He is well noted for his many talents – percussionist, gospel singer, preacher of the gospel, and in the secular world, former over-the-road truck driver, and now an over-the-road motor coach operator, along with his traveling for the Lord preaching the gospel.

In 2001 Bishop Shouse received the mantle of leadership from his father, assuming the role of Presiding Bishop, and under the direction of the Lord has brought the fellowship thus far. Along with the responsibility of the churches in the United States, he is also responsible for the GEFI churches on the continent of Africa.

In December 2002, he was appointed Senior Pastor of the Greater Life Evangelistic Temple, now known as the Temple of Praise, with the motto of, "Praise is what we do!"

In 2004, the International Apostolic University of Grace and Truth, Indianapolis, Indiana, conferred on him an honorary Doctor of Divinity degree.

Bishop Shouse has been united in marriage to Evangelist Rose Marie Lisath for 56 years. They are proud parents of three beautiful children, Loretta, Anissa, Edward Jr., (LaVertta), and the proud grandparents of NeVaeh and

Quander Lear, and a special daughter, Brooklyn Lisath, and many spiritual sons and daughters.

His vision for GEFI is for it to be one of the premier religious fellowships in the world and to continue to lead God's people on to new heights and dimensions in Christ and to bring to pass those things which advance the cause of Christ in the Body of Christ.

Bishop Shouse is known for his humility, humor, friendliness, sincerity, love of all people, and dedication to the Lord. You will often hear him say his motto, *"We're striving for Excellence in the Body of Christ!"*

FOR INFORMATION, CONTACT:

Bishop Edward E. Shouse, Sr., DD
5702 Earnings Dr.
Columbus, OH 43232
614-321-6101
shouseedward@yahoo.com

Follow me on Facebook:

https://www.facebook.com/Bishop-Quander-L-Wilson-Sr-

A-Man-Before-His-Time-107214114473870

www.ingramcontent.com/pod-product-compliance
Lightning Source LLC
Chambersburg PA
CBHW072012090426
42740CB00011B/2156